AMAZING
Uses for
Brand-Name
PRODUCTS

Christine Halvorson

Ken Sheldon

 Publications International, Ltd.

Christine Halvorson is a freelance writer based in Hancock, New Hampshire. She is coauthor of *Clean & Simple: A Back-to-Basics Approach to Cleaning Your Home* and *Ben Franklin's Almanac of Wit, Wisdom and Practical Advice*. She also wrote *Arm & Hammer Baking Soda: 100s of Helpful Hints* and *Solve It With Salt and Vinegar*.

Ken Sheldon is coauthor of *Clean & Simple: A Back-to-Basics Approach to Cleaning Your Home* and *Ben Franklin's Almanac of Wit, Wisdom and Practical Advice*. He has also contributed to numerous publications, including the *Old Farmer's Almanac*.

Illustrations by Jeff Moores.

The brand-name products mentioned in this publication are trademarks owned by their respective companies. Mention of these products in this publication does not constitute an endorsement by these companies with this publication.

This book is for informational purposes and is not intended to provide medical advice. Neither Publications International, Ltd., nor the authors, editors, or publisher, take responsibility for any possible consequences from any treatment, procedure, exercise, dietary modification, action, or application of medication or preparation by any person reading or following the information in this book. The publication of this book does not constitute the practice of medicine, and this book does not attempt to replace your physician or other health care provider. Before undertaking any course of treatment, the authors, editors, and publisher advise the reader to check with a physician or other health care provider.

Before trying any of these uses on fabrics, carpets, flooring, cabinets, and the like, you should refer to the manufacturers' recommended cleaning methods.

Contents

Introduction

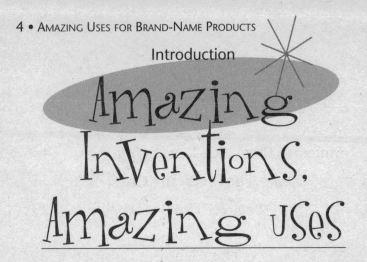

Amazing Inventions, Amazing Uses

Corporate America is full of mythic stories about how one invention inadvertently led to another. For example, the microwave oven was allegedly the result of World War II–era technology and a keen observation by one scientist who noticed his candy bar had melted in his pocket while he was playing around with radar waves. The office must-have Post-it Note was really an industrial accident at the 3M corporation, created when an employee who was trying to come up with a new, stronger glue instead came up with a new, *weaker* one.

The rest is history, and we love it. Entire books have been written on the subject of inventions that were accidents. As a culture, we seem fascinated by these stories of chance consequences that turned out to be gold mines.

In *Amazing Uses for Brand-Name Products,* we present some of the most interesting unintended uses people have come across over the years for the various household products they've had stored under their sinks, in their kitchen cupboards, and out in the garage. You'll find tips that will help you throughout the house and beyond, including tackling musty bathroom mildew, eliminating pests in the garden, fixing up furniture, organizing camping gear, and so much more.

While these tips and tricks aren't quite as complicated as radar waves and the tricky sticky properties of glue, they might come in handy when you find yourself fresh out of one product and really need to complete a task *this instant,* when necessity really is the mother of invention. These tips might also be helpful if you want to change the kinds of chemicals you bring into your house or for folks who may have developed an allergy or a sensitivity to one product or another. It happens.

But we know the real reason you'll want to check out these tips is so you can impress your friends at parties—"Say, did you know you can shave with peanut butter?"

Chapter 1

The Medicine Chest

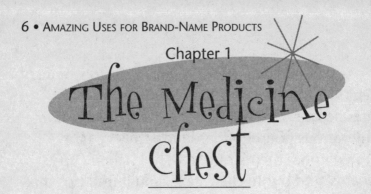

When we have minor aches, pains, scrapes, and complaints, it's easiest to reach into the medicine cabinet and pull out a bottle of something. In a pinch, you can do just as well by reaching into your kitchen cupboard or refrigerator. There you might find the ingredients for tried-and-true

home remedies that can do the job, save you a trip to the local drugstore, and avoid chemicals you would rather not put in or on your body.

THE SKINNY ON SKIN
Become clean cut
Use Scope mouthwash as an astringent to disinfect wounds. Pour it directly onto an abrasion or a laceration.

Try cleaning minor scrapes and bruises with Pampers baby wipes. They're gentle on tender skin.

Use white vinegar to disinfect minor cuts. Pour vinegar on a clean cloth and dab on the wound, applying light pressure to stop the bleeding. Cover with a sterile bandage.

Unbind the bandage
Loosen an adhesive bandage and remove it painlessly by rubbing it with a little Alberto VO5 Conditioning Hairdressing. After a few minutes, peel off the bandage.

Too much fun in the sun
Keeping a sunburn moisturized helps heal the skin. Smooth on bath oil after soaking in a cool tub, then apply Vaseline Intensive Care lotion liberally.

Mix cornstarch and water to make a paste and apply directly on sunburn to soothe the pain.

Cool yogurt, whipped cream, or whole milk can ease sunburn pain. Apply one of these to the sunburn, let sit for 20 minutes, then rinse with lukewarm water.

Banish the burns

Apply Pepsodent toothpaste to soothe a minor burn.

Ease the pain of a minor burn by applying a cold, wet tea bag to the burned area. Keep a wet tea bag in the refrigerator for minor cooking burns.

An oatmeal bath can relieve the itching of minor burns. Add 1 cup plain uncooked oatmeal to a lukewarm bath as the tub fills. Soak in the tub for at least 20 minutes.

Use honey to treat a burn. Place a dab of honey on a sterile gauze bandage and cover the wound. Change the dressing 4 times a day.

Soothe a scalded throat or tongue by taking 2 teaspoons olive oil.

Ate that hot pizza too fast? Instantly cool the roof of your mouth with a squirt of whipped cream.

Rash attacks

Use lemon juice as a home remedy to relieve the itching and alleviate the rash of poison ivy. Apply directly to affected areas.

Calm those itchy hives with milk. Soak a cloth in a bowl of cold milk and apply to the affected area for 10 minutes. Wring out, soak in milk again, and reapply.

Here's a time-tested method for preventing diaper rash: Apply a thin coat of Vaseline Petroleum Jelly to baby's clean, dry bottom before diapering.

 Cornstarch is more absorbent than talcum powder and can be substituted for baby powder. Use sparingly, and be sure to keep it away from baby's nose and eyes.

Stop the sting

Treat insect bites and poison ivy with a mixture of 1 quart milk, 2 tablespoons salt, and ice. Apply with a cloth to affected skin for 20 minutes 3 times daily.

To ease the pain of an insect bite, dip a cloth into a solution of 2 Alka-Seltzer tablets dissolved in a glass of water. Place on the bite for 20 minutes.

A paste made of baking soda and vinegar can also ease the pain of a sting.

Make a soothing paste for a bug bite or sting by combining equal parts salt and baking soda, mixed with a little water. Apply to the affected area with a cotton ball.

Dip a cotton ball in undiluted vinegar and hold against a mosquito bite to relieve the itch.

Rub a little Pepsodent toothpaste onto a mosquito bite or insect sting to soothe the pain and itch.

Soothe frostbite with warm olive oil dabbed gently onto affected skin. Then seek medical attention.

FIXES FOR FEET

Keep your feet dry to avoid athlete's foot. Sprinkle cornstarch on your feet and in your shoes to absorb moisture.

Soak your toes in Scope mouthwash to get rid of unsightly toenail fungus.

Sprinkle cornstarch in your socks before working out to prevent athlete's foot. If you shower at the gym, always wear flip-flops.

ATHLETE'S FOOT HOME REMEDY

Athlete's foot is a fungal infection and thrives in dampness. Try this home remedy for relief: Mix 30 minced garlic cloves, 4 teaspoons ground cinnamon, and 4 teaspoons powdered cloves in ½ cup rubbing alcohol. Put mixture in a sealed jar and let steep for 2 weeks out of sunlight. Apply 2 times a day with cotton balls. Keep feet dry with a dusting of cornstarch.

Dab a few drops of Scope mouthwash on a broken blister to prevent it from getting infected.

HELP FOR WOMEN'S WOES

Eating yogurt daily may reduce the occurrence of yeast infections *(candida vaginitis)*. Be sure the yogurt you eat contains active *lactobacillus acidophilus* cultures.

Yogurt can also be applied directly for yeast infections. Mix 1 cup *plain* (not vanilla) yogurt with 1 teaspoon cinnamon. Use a baster to insert yogurt into the vagina. Be sure yogurt has active *lactobacillus acidophilus* cultures.

After an episiotomy, Pampers baby wipes are gentle enough to use on sensitive areas instead of toilet paper.

URINARY TRACT INFECTION ELIXIR

Make your own elixir to heal or prevent a urinary tract infection. Boil 8 ounces cranberry juice, then reduce heat and add 2 teaspoons powdered Echinacea root. Simmer for 15 minutes. Remove from heat, then add 1 teaspoon powdered goldenseal root. Steep for 20 minutes. Strain and add honey or lemon. Drink warm or iced.

At the onset of symptoms of a urinary tract infection, try this unusual treatment: Dissolve 2 tablets of Alka-Seltzer in a glass of water and drink.

MIND YOUR MOUTH

Cranky canker sores

Soothe a canker sore by coating the area with a gentle swish of Phillips' Milk of Magnesia.

You can speed the healing of canker sores by eating yogurt twice daily until the sores clear. Yogurt also helps soothe the pain.

Cold milk helps speed the healing of a cold sore. Apply a milk-soaked cotton ball to the sore to ease the pain.

Dab a little lemon juice on that irritating cold sore or fever blister. It acts as an astringent and promotes healing.

Tooth troubles
You can stop your gums from bleeding after having a tooth pulled by pressing a moist, cool tea bag against the tooth cavity.

CURES FOR COUGHS AND COLDS
Calm a Cough

Make your own cough syrup: Mix 4 tablespoons lemon juice, 1 cup honey, and ½ cup olive oil. Heat, then stir vigorously. Take 1 teaspoon every 2 hours.

Common kitchen ingredients make an effective cough syrup. Mix ¼ cup honey and ¼ cup apple cider vinegar. Seal in a jar and shake well. Take 1 tablespoon every 4 hours.

Honey promotes the flow of mucus and is great for coughs. Mix 1 tablespoon honey with 1 cup hot water and 2 drops lemon juice. Sip for relief.

FEVER REDUCER

Sip this warm elixir to reduce a fever. Combine 1½ teaspoons cream of tartar, ½ teaspoon lemon juice, 2½ cups warm water, and ½ teaspoon honey. Drink slowly.

CHICKEN SOUP FOR THE COLD

Yes, scientists say, chicken soup does aid colds for a number of reasons:
- The steam from the warm liquid soothes irritated air passageways.
- Chicken soup contains anti-inflammatory properties.
- Cysteines in the soup help thin mucus.
- It can calm coughs associated with colds.

Brew a cup of garlic broth to cure a cough. Add 1 to 3 crushed garlic cloves to 2 quarts water, boil, then simmer for 1 hour. Strain and sip.

Make a healing honey potion for bronchitis. Slice an onion into a bowl, cover with honey, and allow to stand overnight. Take 1 teaspoon of the liquid 4 times a day.

Throat therapy

Drink a warm cup of tea mixed with lemon juice and honey to soothe a sore throat or laryngitis.

To relieve a sore throat mix ¼ cup vinegar with ¼ cup honey and take 1 tablespoon 6 times a day. Vinegar kills bacteria, and honey is soothing.

Stop the stuffiness

A strong peppermint candy or mint might be just the thing to clear up your stuffed nose. Try chewing on a couple to relieve congestion.

Keep winter sniffles at bay by eating ½ cup of yogurt daily before and during cold season.

Spicy or herbal tea is great for colds. Brew a cup with some of these antiviral ingredients: mint, ginger, lemon balm, yarrow, thyme, elder, or bee balm.

Relieve stuffiness with an aromatic chest rub. Combine 10 drops lavender essential oil, 15 drops eucalyptus essential oil, and ¼ cup vegetable oil. Mix and massage.

Ease an earache

To soothe an earache, put warm (not hot) olive oil into a dropper and add a few drops into the ear. Then apply a warm heating pad.

THE LAST STRAW

If you don't have an eyedropper handy, improvise with a GLAD flexible straw. Insert the straw into the liquid, cover the open end with your finger, lift, and use.

TOO SLOW, TOO FAST:
CONSTIPATION AND DIARRHEA
Get moving

Constipated? Try this drink before
breakfast: Mix 1 cup warm water,
4 tablespoons lemon juice, and honey
to taste.

Two tablespoons molasses taken before bedtime
can help keep you regular. Add the molasses to
milk, fruit juice, or even prune juice to dilute the
strong taste.

Here's a gentle and palatable way to ease constipation. Take 1 tablespoon honey (a mild laxative)
3 times a day. Mix with blackstrap molasses for
more punch.

 Vegetable oil lubricates the intestines
and helps to get things moving. Take 2 to
3 tablespoons olive, safflower, or soybean
oil daily until you find relief.

A simple salad dressed with oil and vinegar may provide just the right combina-
tion of fiber and lubricating action to
ease constipation.

Slow it down

Drink plenty of tea and eat toast
to help relieve diarrhea. The liquid will
replace lost fluids, and the tannin in tea
is therapeutic.

Lactobacillus acidophilus in yogurt
restores natural intestinal cultures.
When taking antibiotics, eat yogurt with
these active cultures to prevent diarrhea
and avoid killing healthful intestinal bacteria.

Eating yogurt can also help cure a case of diarrhea. Yogurt helps produce lactic acid in your
intestines, which can kill the nasty bacteria that
is the source of the problem.

INDIGESTION AND OVERINDULGENCE

Hangover cure

Caffeine reduces the swelling of
blood vessels that cause headaches.
To relieve a hangover, try drinking
a couple cups of strong coffee.

Unsettled stomachs

Try this elixir as a remedy for nausea: Mix 1 cup
water, 10 drops lime juice, and ½ teaspoon sugar.
Then add ¼ teaspoon baking soda, and drink.

Bland foods ease nausea, hence the wisdom of this Indian folk remedy: Cover a bowl of un-buttered, unsalted popcorn (popped without oil) with boiling water. Eat the resulting mush slowly.

Burps and gurgles

Eat yogurt with live cultures to help restore intestinal balance and reduce acids that lead to heartburn.

Ordinary soda crackers digest easily and absorb stomach acid because they contain cream of tartar and bicarbonate of soda. Chew them for heartburn.

Make a tasty compote of baked pumpkin and apples spiced with cinnamon and honey to get rid of heartburn. Or, eat the fresh, baked pump-kin by itself.

The effervescence of club soda soothes indigestion. The bubbles make you burp, providing relief.

This fizzy drink helps neutralize stomach acid: Mix 10 drops lime juice with ½ teaspoon sugar, then add ¼ teaspoon baking soda. Drink as soon as it fizzes.

Cream of tartar is an acid neutralizer. Mix ½ teaspoon with ½ teaspoon baking soda in a glass of water and drink to ease heartburn.

REAR TROUBLES

Here's how to relieve hemorrhoid pain: Make a paste of cornstarch and water, gradually adding more water to measure a pint. Boil, then cool completely and use in an enema.

To avoid aggravating sensitive hemorrhoids, use soothing Pampers baby wipes instead of toilet paper.

SPRAINS, STRAINS, AND "OH, MY ACHING ____"

Massage the pain away

A Penn tennis ball inside of a sock makes an excellent massager for the lower back.

You can also roll the bottoms of your feet over Penn tennis balls while you sit in a chair.

Make your own massage oil to soothe sore muscles. Mix 1 tablespoon horse-radish in ½ cup olive oil and let mixture stand for 30 minutes. Apply liberally.

To soothe arthritis pain in your hands, make a paste by mixing 2 cups oatmeal and 1 cup water in a bowl. Warm (but don't cook) the mixture, then apply for quick relief.

ICE PACKS TO FIT YOUR FORM

• Keep ice packs in the freezer for the occasional sprain or aching muscle. To make a small ice pack, pour 1 cup rubbing alcohol and 2 cups water into a quart-size GLAD Zipper Bag. Squeeze out air and press closed. The mixture will remain slushy, which is helpful for shaping around sprained knees or elbows. For large ice packs, use gallon GLAD Zipper Bags and double the recipe.

• You can also freeze unpopped popcorn in small GLAD Zipper Bags for bumps and bruises. Refreeze as necessary.

• A package of frozen peas or corn can be used as an emergency ice pack.

• Keep a wet O-Cel-O sponge in the freezer, dampen, and apply to the sore area.

Relieve bursitis by massaging the shoulder or upper arm with warm vegetable oil daily.

OTHER TRICKS AND TIPS
Sweet dreams
Honey has a mild sedative effect and can aid sleep. Add to herbal tea or warm milk before bedtime.

A Penn tennis ball can prevent snoring. Sew it inside a pocket on the back of your pajama top to keep yourself from sleeping on your back.

Splinter relief
You can remove a splinter more easily by first soaking the affected area in corn oil to soften the skin.

For a pesky splinter, squeeze a drop of Elmer's glue over the splinter, let dry, and peel off. The splinter will stick to the glue.

Break the habit

Ease nicotine withdrawal symptoms by drinking 2 Alka-Seltzer tablets dissolved in a glass of water at each meal. Avoid this if you're on a low-sodium diet or have peptic ulcers.

Perk up

Give yourself more energy with a spoonful of blackstrap molasses, known in folk medicine as a "blood builder." One tablespoon contains 3.5 mg of iron.

Pill problems

If you have difficulty swallowing pills, try rolling them in softened butter first. This will make them slide down more smoothly.

Use clear Revlon Nail Enamel as a do-it-yourself laminate to keep prescription labels clear and readable. Paint the polish directly on the label.

Use red Revlon Nail Enamel to paint the arrows or markings on child-proof medicine bottles. It will help you line them up quickly and easily.

Chapter 2

The Beauty Shop

Mayonnaise, lemon juice, milk. These food staples lurking in your refrigerator or kitchen cupboards are the same ingredients used in many proven beauty secrets. Explore these innovative ways to pamper your body and soul—and your hair, face, and skin while you're at it. You may just uncover a hidden highlight in your hair, a surface shine to your skin, and a new bounce in your step.

A BOOST FOR YOUR BODY
Beauty baths

Suave shampoo can be used as a bubble bath. Pour a capful into running water as you fill the tub.

Mix 3 tablespoons Suave shampoo and 2 cups vegetable oil in a blender. Use as a moisturizing bubble bath.

SCENTED BUBBLING BATH MIX

2 cups vegetable oil
3 tablespoons Suave shampoo
2 to 3 drops perfume

Pour ingredients into a blender and mix well for 10 seconds. Store in a plastic bottle, and add 2 tablespoons to each bath.

Add ½ cup baking soda to bathwater to help relieve sore muscles and fatigue.

Make yourself a soothing milk bath by adding ½ cup dry milk powder to warm bathwater. Milk soothes the skin.

Perfume power

A little dab of Vaseline Petroleum Jelly rubbed over your wrist or neck where you've put perfume or cologne will help the scent last longer.

Dip a few Q-Tip Cotton Swabs in your favorite fragrance—either perfume, cologne, or a scented oil—and carry them in your purse, sealed in a GLAD Zipper Bag. Touch a Q-Tip to a few pressure points later in the day or whenever you need a pick-me-up.

FACE VALUE
Eye appeal

After applying mascara, dip a Q-Tip Cotton Swab in a little Johnson's Baby Powder and sweep it over your lashes. Then apply a second coat of mascara. Lashes will appear longer and fuller.

To remove errant eye shadow flecks from your face, use a Q-Tip. It will remove specks without ruining your foundation.

Dab a bit of olive or vegetable oil to the crow's feet around your eyes at night.

HAPPY SKIN

- Look no further than your kitchen cupboards for excellent skin moisturizers: Safflower oil, margarine, mayonnaise, and vegetable oil all work well.
- Remove flaky skin by dipping a cotton ball or pad in milk and applying it to the flaky patch. Rinse with cool water.
- Use mayonnaise as a treatment for those really tough, rough, dry spots on the skin, such as feet, knees, and elbows. Rub a dab of mayo into the spot, then rinse clean.
- If you're sitting in an air-conditioned space or a steam-heated room, use extra layers of Vaseline Intensive Care hand lotion to prevent skin from drying out.

Keep an emergency eye-relief kit in the freezer. Dip Q-Tip Cotton Swabs into cool water and store them in a small GLAD Zipper Bag in the freezer. To relieve tired eyes, roll the Q-Tips under your eyes to reduce puffiness.

Luscious lips

Vaseline Petroleum Jelly can be applied directly to lips with a fingertip as protection against wind and cold and to soften lips overnight. Apply some to hands, too.

Makeup removal magic

In a GLAD Zipper Bag, place a few Q-Tip Cotton Swabs and your favorite makeup remover in a small container. Carry it with you for emergency makeup fixes, such as smeared mascara or lipstick.

Use Vaseline Petroleum Jelly to remove makeup, including lipstick, mascara, blush, and founda-tion. Be sure to wash off any excess Vaseline.

Dry milk can be used as a makeup remover. Mix 1 teaspoon milk powder with warm water and apply to your face using a cotton ball. Rinse clean.

KID CLEANUP

- A quick trick to remove stains on your kids' faces is to rub the spots off with Pepsodent toothpaste. Rinse thoroughly.
- Clean that stubbornly dirty area behind kids' ears by rubbing in a generous amount of Vaseline Petroleum Jelly with a dry cloth.
- Spread Vaseline Petroleum Jelly above a baby's eyes and across his or her forehead to prevent shampoo from getting into eyes during a bath.
- If your child gets gum or some other sticky substance in his or her hair, work it free by rubbing it with Vaseline Petroleum Jelly.

 Use Alberto VO5 Conditioning Hairdressing to remove makeup. Apply a little to a cotton ball and wipe clean.

After removing your makeup, apply plain yogurt to your face just as you would a liquid soap. Rinse thoroughly. Yogurt helps rebalance your skin's pH.

Use whipped cream to remove your face makeup at night. First splash your face with warm water, then spread whipped cream over skin. Rinse with warm water, and dry.

Bye-bye, blemishes

 After your usual facial-cleansing routine, apply Phillips' Milk of Magnesia with a cotton ball or pad to any acne blemishes. Let dry, then rinse off using cool water.

Apply lemon juice to blackheads using a cotton ball or a Q-Tip Cotton Swab. Leave the juice on overnight. In the morning, rinse your face with cool water. Repeat every night for 1 week.

For acne outbreaks, apply lemon juice on a Q-Tip Cotton Swab several times a day to dry up pimples more quickly.

Spread mayonnaise over your face and let it dry for 20 minutes. Rinse off with warm water, then follow with a cold water splash. This treatment will help tighten pores.

 Scope mouthwash can improve acne. Dab the mouthwash on blemishes with a cotton ball.

Honey speeds healing by killing bacteria. For an overnight blemish remedy, dab honey on the spot and cover with a bandage.

If you're suffering from a boil, make a compress with tomato paste and cover the boil. The acids in the paste will bring the boil to a head and relieve the pain.

 A dab of Pepsodent toothpaste on pimples will help clear them up overnight. Use as you would any acne ointment.

Face-loving facials

This treatment works well for normal to dry skin: Mash ½ of a banana in a bowl. Add 1 tablespoon honey and 2 tablespoons sour cream; mix well. Apply to your face, leave on for 10 minutes, then rinse with warm water.

Spread plain yogurt in a thin layer over your face and allow it to dry. When dry, rinse with lukewarm water.

Mix 1 tablespoon dry milk, ½ of a peeled cucumber, and 1 teaspoon plain yogurt. Apply to face, let dry, and rinse.

COMBINATION SKIN MASQUE

Separate an egg, saving the white in a bowl and the yolk in another bowl. Beat each separately. Apply the egg white to oily areas and the yolk to dry areas of your face. Allow to dry for 20 minutes, then rinse off with warm water.

Make your own facial scrub by adding 1 teaspoon sugar to your favorite liquid face cleanser in your hand. Apply to face gently. This will help remove dead skin cells.

More moisture

Use a tube of Blistex Lip Balm as a face moisturizer. Just rub it over your face when you're out in the cold.

Olive oil makes an excellent facial moisturizer. Apply a few drops with a cotton ball. Do not rinse off.

Moisten a dry-skinned face by applying whipped cream and letting it dry on your face for 30 minutes. Rinse off with warm water.

RUSTPROOFING IN THE BATHROOM

Rustproof the bottom of your shaving cream can by painting the edges with clear Revlon Nail Enamel.

After washing your face, leave it slightly damp and apply Vaseline Petroleum Jelly with your fingertips. Spread it evenly and thinly to protect and moisturize your skin.

Clean shavin'

Who needs shaving cream when you can shave your face or legs with peanut butter? (We recommend not using the crunchy style.) Other shaving cream stand-ins: vegetable oil, whipped cream, Vaseline Intensive Care hand lotion, and Suave hair conditioner.

Next time you're careless while shaving, dab Blistex Lip Balm on the nick.

NEAT TREATS FOR HANDS AND FEET
Drastic cleaning measures

Tar stuck to bare feet can be removed by rubbing them with Pepsodent toothpaste.

Use vegetable oil or Johnson's Baby Oil to take paint off your hands after a household painting project. Both products are gentler on your hands than turpentine.

Gillette shaving cream works as well as soap to clean your hands. This may be an excellent choice if you need waterless cleaning, such as when you're camping or hiking.

Odor out

If you have a lingering smell on your hands from onions, fish, or other strong-smelling foods, rub them with a bit of Pepsodent toothpaste. Rinse.

SOOTHING FOOT TREATMENT

Warm some vegetable oil in a double boiler or set a glass measuring cup inside a pan of water on the stove. Apply the warm oil to your feet, wrap them in a warm damp towel, and sit for 10 minutes or until the towel cools off.

To eliminate stubborn foot odors, add 4 tea bags to 1 quart boiling water. Pour into a wash basin and add enough cold water to cool off the mixture and cover feet. Soak feet for ½ hour. Dry thoroughly, and apply foot powder. Repeat twice a day, if necessary, until problem disappears.

All dried up

Repair cracked and chapped feet or hands by covering them with a thin layer of Vaseline Petroleum Jelly, then wearing cotton socks or gloves while you sleep.

TIPS FOR HAIR, THERE, AND EVERYWHERE

Detangle the tangles

To help comb out snarled hair between shampoos, mix Suave hair conditioner with water. Store mixture in a spray bottle, and spritz on when hair needs a little help to detangle.

Dandruff duty

Prevent dandruff by dabbing Scope mouthwash on your scalp with a cotton ball. Leave on for 30 minutes; shampoo normally.

Lemon juice can also attack dandruff. First, rub 1 tablespoon lemon juice into dry hair. Shampoo and rinse as usual. Next, mix 2 tablespoons lemon juice into 2 cups water; rinse hair again. Repeat on alternate days for 1 week.

DANDRUFF-CONTROL HOT OIL TREATMENT

Pour 2 or 3 tablespoons olive oil into a glass measuring cup (do not use nontempered glass), and place the cup in a pan of water. Warm the water slowly on a stove to heat the oil. When the oil is warmed, dab it onto your hair at the scalp using cotton balls. Divide your hair into small sections to get maximum coverage. Massage lightly. Leave the oil on several hours, then shampoo and rinse thoroughly.

Uncommon conditioning

Condition your hair by applying mayonnaise before shampooing. Apply to dry hair and let sit for ½ hour, then rinse and shampoo as usual.

Swimmers can avoid damage to hair from chlorinated water by applying a little Vaseline Petroleum Jelly to their hair before swimming.

To condition your hair naturally, apply ½ cup mayonnaise to dry, unwashed hair. Cover with a plastic bag and leave on for 15 minutes. Rinse a few times before shampooing thoroughly.

Final Touch fabric softener can be used just as you would any hair conditioner after a shampoo.

HELP FOR DAMAGED HAIR

Repair damaged hair by treating it with oil and egg yolk. Massage olive oil into hair. Then beat the yolk of 1 egg and massage it into hair, working from the ends up. Leave on for 10 minutes, then shampoo as usual. Do this once a week for a month and hair should begin to feel healthier.

Use whipped cream as a hair conditioner. Apply whipped cream to hair and leave on for ½ hour. Rinse thoroughly, then shampoo as usual.

Residue removers

Beer can remove residue from your hair. Add 6 tablespoons beer to 1 cup warm water, and pour it over your hair as a final rinse.

If your hair is prone to buildup from conditioners, styling gel, or hair spray, mix 1 tablespoon baking soda with your regular shampoo once a week. Rinse and dry as usual.

Cool coloring tricks

Before undertaking an at-home hair coloring project, spread Vaseline Petroleum Jelly all around the base of your scalp, above your eyebrows, and around your ears. This will prevent coloring from getting on your skin or in your eyes.

Blonde highlights will magically appear if you rinse your hair with a mixture of ¼ cup lemon juice and ¾ cup water.

Golden highlights come through in red or brown hair when rinsed with brewed tea. Make enough tea to thoroughly rinse through hair after shampooing, then dry as usual.

Bring out the shiny highlights in brown or red hair by rinsing it with coffee. Brew 2 or 3 strong cups (enough to cover your hair) and let it cool. Then pour this into your hair after shampooing. No need to rinse.

Dyed blonde hair has a tendency to take on a greenish tint with too much swimming in a chlorinated pool. To undo the green, rinse your hair with club soda.

Another treatment for removing a greenish tint in blonde hair is tomato juice. Rub enough into your hair to cover it, leave on 2 minutes, then rinse thoroughly.

HAIRBRUSH HELP

To clean those nasty hairbrushes, fill your bathroom sink with warm water and add a capful of Suave shampoo. Soak your hairbrushes and combs in this for ½ hour, then rinse thoroughly.

Hair emergency measures

If your hair is dirty and you don't have time to shampoo it, pour cornstarch into the palm of your hand and rub it through your hair at the scalp. Brush through your hair until the powder is no longer visible.

If your hair is flying all over the place because of static electricity, apply a little Vaseline Petroleum Jelly to your comb or brush and run it through your hair.

Quirky setting gels

 Dissolve 1 teaspoon instant gelatin powder in a cup of warm water and use this mixture as a hair gel. This is great to apply before rolling in curlers or before shaping today's styles with your fingers.

Keep errant eyebrows or mustaches in place by applying a little Blistex Lip Balm and styling with your fingertips.

A MANICURIST'S ADVICE
Nail nonsense

You can use Krazy Glue to repair a split or torn fingernail in an emergency.

Use a tea bag and clear Revlon Nail Enamel to repair a badly broken nail. Just cut a small piece out of the tea bag, cover the tear, then apply the polish to the fabric. Press gently and repolish the nail with a colored polish.

Happy, healthy nails

Keeping your cuticles moisturized will prevent hangnails. Apply Vaseline Intensive Care hand lotion to cuticles using a Q-Tip Cotton Swab.

Soak your fingernails in lemon juice for 10 minutes, then rinse well with warm water. This will help strengthen and brighten fingernails.

Perfect polishing

Use a Q-Tip Cotton Swab to fix smudges on cuticles or edges when polishing your nails. If you need a really sharp point, tease the end of the Q-Tip and twist it into a point before dabbing.

Before capping your nail polish bottle, use a Q-Tip to apply a thin coat of Vaseline Petroleum Jelly to the threads inside of the cap. This will prevent the cap from getting stuck.

Chapter 3

The Cleaning Cabinet

Cleaning your home is a constant battle, a bit of a bore, and, generally speaking, no fun at all. You just do it. In fact, you've probably been doing certain chores for decades without even thinking about *how* you do them or *why* you use certain products. In this chapter, you may find a sneaky way to get an unpleasant task done quicker or a new cleaning trick that might save you money, time, energy— or all three!

BATTLING THE BATHROOM
Toilet scrubbing schemes

Give your toilet an overnight cleaning by putting ¼ cup 20 Mule Team Borax in the bowl and letting it sit overnight. In the morning, scrub stains away.

 You can achieve the same effect overnight by putting 2 Polident Denture Cleanser tablets in the toilet and letting them sit overnight. Scrub the toilet in the morning.

The citric acid and bubbling action of Alka-Seltzer tablets can work to clean your toilet. Drop 2 tablets in the bowl, wait 20 minutes, then brush clean.

Dump a can of flat cola in your toilet bowl, let it sit for 1 hour, then scrub.

Hairy business

Remove hair buildup from your bathtub drain or trap with a Q-Tip Cotton Swab. Just dip it into the drain, twirl, and toss.

TOILET BOWL CLEANER

Use Tide Powder detergent combined with baking soda for a homemade toilet bowl cleaner. Just mix 1 cup baking soda with 1 cup Tide. Each time you clean, sprinkle ¼ cup of this mixture into the toilet and let it sit 10 minutes. Scrub briefly, then let it sit another 10 minutes. Brush again, then flush. When stubborn stains are a problem, drop Tide directly onto the stain and scrub.

Clear a slow drain by dropping in a couple of Alka-Seltzer tablets. Pour in 1 cup vinegar, then flush with hot water.

Save your shower curtains

Help plastic shower curtain hooks glide more easily by applying a thin coat of Alberto VO5 Conditioning Hairdressing to the shower curtain rod.

 Add a few drops of Johnson's Baby Oil to the rinse water when you clean a plastic shower curtain. The oil will keep the curtain more flexible.

Crummy soap scum

Add 1 cup Final Touch fabric softener to 1 quart warm water and use to loosen and clean soap scum from shower doors.

TOUGH TUB CLEANING

When rust or other stains just won't come out of a white porcelain tub with average scrubbing (a common problem with older and antique tubs), add enough water to 20 Mule Team Borax to make a paste. Make sure it's sticky enough to adhere to the sides of the tub. Apply the paste onto stubborn stains using a paint or pastry brush, and cover with a damp Scott Towel. Let sit 1 hour, then scrub with a nylon dish scrubber or a scrubbing brush.

UNCLOGGING SHOWERHEADS

If you have a clogged showerhead that is also too stubborn to come apart, make a soaking bag for it by filling a GLAD Zipper Bag with white vinegar. Wrap the filled bag around the showerhead and attach it to the pipes with a rubber band. Let it sit overnight, and by morning the head should come loose (even if it doesn't, any mineral deposits should be dissolved).

 Use a Downy Sheet to help remove soap scum from shower doors. Wipe across the scum and toss.

Mix 1 part Johnson's Baby Oil with 4 parts water in a clean, empty spray bottle. Spray on soap scum and dirt in your shower or tub. Wipe off with a sponge.

Powdered Electrasol Automatic Dish-washing Detergent makes a great cleaner for removing rings around the tub. Using a wet sponge, sprinkle on the rings and wipe.

Apply a coat of Simoniz Original Paste Wax to the doors of your fiberglass shower stall to prevent soap buildup and to make cleaning easier.

Coat the tile walls of your bathroom shower with Pledge furniture polish to prevent soap scum buildup and water spots.

No more mildew

Use Clorox Bleach to clean grungy caulking around a bathtub or shower. Just mix ¾ cup bleach with 1 gallon water, and scrub the caulk with a toothbrush dipped in this solution. (Always wear rubber gloves when cleaning with bleach.)

Mildew can build up on your shower and tub accessories. Mix 1½ cups Clorox Bleach with 2 gallons water and scrub bath mats, curtains, and soap dishes with the mixture, using a sponge or scrub brush. Rinse.

CLEAN CLEANING SUPPLIES

Revitalize old, smelly sponges by soaking them for 10 minutes in Clorox Bleach and water. Mix ¾ cup bleach with 1 gallon water. Be sure to rinse thoroughly afterward.

Full-strength Rite Aid rubbing alcohol can remove small areas of mildew buildup on grout, caulk, or tile. Dip a cloth into the alcohol and scrub the spot.

If your bathroom never seems to be fully dry and you are going away for some time, place a large, shallow box of Fresh Step cat litter in your bathtub to absorb moisture.

Goodbye yellow, hello white

Make a paste of salt and turpentine and use to whiten yellowed porcelain tubs or sinks. Wearing rubber gloves, apply the mixture with a stiff brush, then rinse thoroughly.

GLOVES SLIDE ON

If you're planning to wear rubber gloves for any cleaning task, first drop a little cornstarch into your palm and rub your hands together to make the gloves easy to slide on.

 Brighten porcelain fixtures with club soda. Spray or drip the soda onto the fixtures and rub with a soft cloth to shine.

See ya later, lime deposits

Use full-strength Rite Aid hydrogen peroxide on lime buildup on your bathroom fixtures. Rinse.

SHINY, HAPPY KITCHEN
Operation: clean oven

Oven racks that have stubborn baked-on black-ened areas can be cleaned by "steaming" off the soot with ammonia vapors. Just lay the racks on old towels in your bathtub. Fill the tub with warm water and ½ cup ammonia, and let it sit ½ hour. Be sure the bathroom is well ventilated. Rinse.

 If a pie or similar sugary item boils over in your oven, sprinkle the sticky spill with salt. Let it sit until the spilled area becomes crisp, then lift off with a spatula when the oven cools.

When cleaning your oven, finish by wiping the entire surface with a sponge using a mixture of equal parts white vinegar and water. This will help prevent grease buildup.

Microwave magic

Loosen encrusted dirt from the inside of a microwave oven by adding 4 tablespoons white vinegar to 1 cup water in a glass measuring cup. Place the cup in the microwave and heat to boiling. After it boils, turn off the microwave, but let the cup sit inside for 5 to 10 minutes. The steam loosens the dirt, making it easy to wipe clean.

Fresh fridge

Fill a small bowl with instant coffee crystals and place it on a back shelf in your refrigerator or freezer to control odor buildup.

 Use vanilla extract and an O-Cel-O sponge to wipe the inside of your refrigerator to deodorize it.

Help your refrigerator shelves stay clean or make them easier to wipe clean by coating them with Simoniz Original Paste Wax.

To clean sticky refrigerator door gaskets, mix 4 tablespoons baking soda with 1 quart water, and apply with a toothbrush. Wipe clean. This helps control mildew buildup, too.

Make use of a ruined pair of No nonsense panty hose by using them to clean under your refrigerator. Wrap the nylon around a yard stick, then run it under the refrigerator.

A+ APPLIANCES

A Q-Tip Cotton Swab can be used to clean the hard-to-reach places on your kitchen blender, electric mixer, or electric can opener. Dip the Q-Tip (or a toothbrush) in warm, soapy water, then scrub and rinse.

KITCHEN WALL CLEANER

Keep this homemade concoction on hand to use for removing grease from the painted walls in your kitchen, especially that area above the stove.

¼ cup baking soda or 20 Mule Team Borax
½ cup white vinegar
1 cup ammonia
1 gallon warm water

Combine ingredients in a large bucket. Save any leftover in plastic spray bottles. Sponge or spray on greasy walls, then rinse thoroughly.

If you'll be away for a weekend getaway, deodorize your refrigerator while you're gone by pouring a little Fresh Step cat litter onto a cookie sheet. Place the sheet on the middle shelf of your refrigerator. Discard upon your return.

Dishwasher delight

Clean out hard-water stains, deodorize, and sparkle the inside of your dishwasher by running a wash load using powdered lemonade mix instead of detergent. The ascorbic acid in the powder helps the cleaning action.

Dispose of disposal odors

Remove odors from your garbage disposal by pouring Clorox Bleach down the drain. Then run hot water for 2 minutes.

Households with septic tanks should deodorize the garbage disposal with ½ cup baking soda and 1 cup vinegar. Let sit 20 minutes, then briefly run hot water.

DRIP STOPPER

Make a bracelet to wear when you are washing ceilings or walls to prevent the wash water from trickling down your arms. Shape an O-Cel-O sponge around your wrist and attach it with a large rubber band.

Sparkling stovetops

Use club soda to clean your stovetops, kitchen counters, and stainless-steel fixtures. Just pour it directly on an O-Cel-O sponge and wipe. Rinse with warm water, then dry thoroughly.

Spray a painted or wallpapered wall behind your stove with Pledge furniture polish and buff it with a soft cloth. This prevents any grease splatters from sticking to the wall.

Mix 1 tablespoon Dawn Dishwashing Detergent with ½ cup household ammonia and enough water to fill a clean spray bottle. Use this mixture to cut grease and clean stovetops, counters, appliances, and any greasy surface. Store the cleaning solution for future use, but make sure to label the bottle.

 Use a Downy Sheet to wipe away grease splatters from the stovetop.

Terrific tile

Rub ceramic tile countertops or walls with Simoniz Original Paste Wax on a soft cloth. Let stand 10 minutes, then buff.

Spiffy sinks

Make a paste out of lemon juice and salt to the consistency of toothpaste, and apply this to brass, copper, or stainless-steel kitchen sinks and sink fixtures. Scrub gently, then rinse with water.

Shine a stainless-steel sink by wiping the surface with a little Alberto VO5 Conditioning Hairdressing. Be sure to use a soft cloth.

After cleaning your stainless-steel kitchen sink, keep it shining by wiping it with vegetable oil.

 Loosen mineral deposits on faucets by sponging on lemon juice, letting it soak for a while, then scrubbing off.

Remove built-up crud on your rubber sink mat by soaking it in the sink. Add ¼ cup Clorox Bleach and fill the sink with water. Let sit 10 minutes, drain, then rinse everything thoroughly.

Primping pots and pans

Burned-on grease in a pot or pan can be removed by filling the pan with water then adding 6 Alka-Seltzer tablets. Let the pan soak for at least 1 hour, then scrub it clean.

Remove baked-on food from a pan by soaking it overnight in water with a Downy Sheet added. The softener helps loosen the food. Wipe clean in the morning.

 Add 1 heaping tablespoon Electrasol Automatic Dishwashing Detergent to a sink filled with hot water. Soak pots and pans with baked-on food overnight, then clean.

White vinegar can help get the stains out of your aluminum pans. Put 2 tablespoons vinegar in the pan, add water to fill, then boil for 10 minutes. The stains should disappear.

Cookware cleanup

 Enamel cookware can't handle abrasive cleaners. Apply a paste made with baking soda and water, and let it sit 1 hour. Then clean with a synthetic scrubber, and rinse.

To clean scratches in stoneware, apply a baking-soda paste to the cracks. Let stand a few minutes, then wash as usual.

Plastic power

To get rid of red tomato stains on your plastic containers and utensils, make a paste using baking soda and water. Mix to the consistency of toothpaste and apply to the stained areas. Let dry, then rub off.

Avoid red tomato stains on plastic by spraying the container with Pam cooking spray before adding tomato-base food. When washing the container, start with cold water, then wash as usual.

Coat your rubber or plastic drain board with Pledge furniture polish. This will prevent stains from setting into the surface.

Clean stains and odors out of a thermos bottle by dropping in 2 tablespoons Electrasol Automatic Dishwashing Detergent and letting it sit for 30 minutes. Swish the bottle, using a bottle brush if necessary, then rinse thoroughly.

 Deodorize and clean a thermos by dropping in 3 Polident Denture Cleanser tablets, fill with water, and let soak for an hour. Rinse thoroughly.

Washing wood

Wash your wood cutting board with lemon juice to help get rid of garlic, onion, or fish smells.

Clorox Bleach can be used to keep butcher-block cutting boards free of bacteria. Wash the cutting board in hot sudsy water and rinse thoroughly. Then mix 3 tablespoons Clorox Bleach with 1 gallon warm water. Soak or brush the solution onto the cutting board, keep it moist for at least 2 minutes, then rinse thoroughly.

Keep wooden spoons, cutting boards, and butcher blocks well oiled by rubbing them with vegetable oil, using a Scott Towel. Wipe away any excess.

Glistening glassware

Soak stained china cups in a mild solution of 1 tablespoon Clorox Bleach and 1 gallon water. This will also make glasses and flatware shine.

You can rub out tiny scratches on your glassware by using a dab of Pepsodent toothpaste.

Remove coffee and tea stains from glassware items by soaking the glassware in a solution of 2 quarts warm water and 2 tablespoons Electrasol Automatic Dishwashing Detergent.

Slick silverware

 Coat silver items with a thin film of Alberto VO5 Conditioning Hairdressing to prevent tarnishing. Wash before using.

Make a paste of cornstarch and water and apply to tarnished silverware. Let dry; wipe clean with a dry cloth.

Mix a solution of 5 ounces dry milk powder, 12 ounces water, and 1 tablespoon white vinegar. Pour this into a 9×13-inch cake pan. Drop in your tarnished silverware and let it sit overnight. In the morning, rinse clean, and dry all pieces thoroughly.

Place 1 or 2 pieces Crayola Chalk in your silverware chest to prevent tarnishing.

Use Pepsodent toothpaste to polish your silverware. First, coat the silverware with toothpaste, then dip each piece into warm water and rub with your fingertips. The toothpaste may actually foam up. Rinse thoroughly, and dry.

FEEL-GOOD LIVING SPACES
Wow 'em walls and woodwork

Cold brewed tea is an excellent cleaner for woodwork. Just dip a clean, soft cloth in the tea and wipe the wood surface.

Mix 2 tablespoons Dawn Dishwashing Detergent with 1 gallon warm water. Use this solution to wipe painted woodwork clean.

Take a grease spot off wallpaper by first blotting it with a Scott Towel, then sprinkling it with cornstarch. Gently rub off the cornstarch, then vacuum the area using the upholstery brush.

 Rub mayonnaise into white water marks on wood paneling. Leave the mayonnaise on the marks overnight, then wipe clean.

Remove crayon marks and drawings from painted walls by rubbing them with white Pepsodent toothpaste on a soft cloth. Rinse away with warm water.

Doing windows, the easy way

You can use Melitta coffee filters of any size to polish your windows or other glass surfaces. They are absorbent, lint-free, handy, and inexpensive.

Window shades that can't be washed using liquid will come clean by rubbing with a terry cloth towel dipped in cornmeal.

If the cords, tapes, or other decorative fabric pieces on your white venetian blinds are gray, touch them up with white Griffin Liquid Wax Shoe Polish.

You can prevent dust from settling on your venetian blinds in the first place by wiping them with Downy Sheets. This helps eliminate static electricity, which attracts dust.

HOMEMADE GLASS CLEANER

2 tablespoons ammonia
½ cup Rite Aid rubbing alcohol
¼ teaspoon Dawn Dishwashing Detergent

Add all ingredients to a spray bottle, then fill the bottle with water and shake well. You can substitute 3 tablespoons vinegar or lemon juice for the ammonia. Use as you would any commercial window cleaner.

Swabbing your decks

Use Dawn Dishwashing Detergent as a quick cleanup for spills on a vinyl kitchen floor. Just dip your sponge in the liquid and wipe.

Pepsodent toothpaste removes black scuff marks on vinyl or linoleum floors. Rub the paste into the mark and wipe away with a damp cloth. A little baking soda added to the toothpaste provides scrubbing power.

Spray Pledge furniture polish on your broom to help keep dust and dirt from flying away when you sweep.

When damp-mopping your vinyl floor, add 1 cup Final Touch fabric softener to ½ pail water to keep the floor shining.

Final Touch fabric softener works to keep special floor types shiny, without buildup of cleaning products. Mix 1 cup fabric softener with ½ gallon warm water and use to clean asphalt, marble, rubber, or terrazzo floors.

Clean and deodorize smelly floor mops by soaking them for a bit in a gallon bucket of water mixed with ¾ cup Clorox Bleach.

Magic carpet cleaning

Mix 1 cup 20 Mule Team Borax with 2 cups cornmeal. Sprinkle this on a smelly carpet. After 1 hour, vacuum.

Add baking soda to the bag in your vacuum to fight smells.

Cover stains or burns in your carpeting with a matching color Crayola Crayon. Rub it into the spot, cover with Reynolds Cut-Rite Wax Paper, and lightly iron on low heat.

CARPET CLEANER

This mixture is good for basic cleaning of nongreasy stains. Combine ¼ teaspoon Dawn Dishwashing Detergent with 1 cup lukewarm water and blot onto the stain until it is gone. Rinse well and blot with Scott Towels until dry.

Blot up a fresh coffee spill on your carpet with a Pampers baby wipe, which is absorbent and nongreasy, so it won't add to the stain.

Pour a bit of club soda on a red wine stain in your carpet. Let it soak a few minutes, then wipe up with an O-Cel-O sponge.

To eliminate static shocks from your carpeting, add a capful of Final Touch fabric softener to a clean, empty spray bottle. Fill with water, shake, and lightly spray on carpets. Do not saturate.

Another emergency spot cleaner for carpeting is Gillette shaving cream. Work into the stain and rinse and blot thoroughly.

Remove tar or other stubborn sticky stuff from carpet fibers by rubbing vegetable oil into the substance. Rub the substance loose, then blot with a Scott Towel.

Revitalizing wood furniture

After polishing any wood furniture in your home, sprinkle a bit of cornstarch over the surface, then use a clean, soft cloth to buff it to a high shine. Any excess oil will be absorbed by the cornstarch.

Clean oak or mahogany furniture by wiping it with warm beer on a soft cloth.

Cool brewed tea can be used to polish varnished wood furniture. Soak a clean cloth in the tea, then wipe.

 Downy Sheets can be used as dust cloths.

Hide small scratches in your wood furniture by rubbing them with a little bit of Alberto VO5 Conditioning Hairdressing and a clean cloth.

Apply mayonnaise to the white rings or spots on your wood furniture, let it sit for 1 hour, then wipe off with a soft cloth and polish.

Rub a bit of cream-style Pepsodent toothpaste into white spots on oil-finished wood furniture. Use a soft cloth and buff the mark away.

Use Vaseline Petroleum Jelly to remove white or dark rings left on wood furniture by damp glasses. Rub the area with the Vaseline, let sit for 24 hours, then wipe with a clean cotton cloth.

Vegetable oil can be used to remove white spots on wood furniture. Dip a cloth into the oil, then into some cigar or cigarette ashes. Rub the cloth with the grain of the wood until spot disappears.

FURNITURE POLISH

In a glass jar with a tight-fitting lid, mix ¼ cup fresh or bottled lemon juice with ½ cup vegetable oil. Apply to wood furniture with a cotton cloth, rubbing in a small amount at a time. This mixture can be stored for several months in a plastic or glass jar, kept out of direct sunlight.

 A little butter folded up into a rag can help rub out a white spot on wood furniture.

Decals, price tags, and stuck-on paper can be removed from wood surfaces by saturating the surface with vegetable oil. Let it sit 10 minutes, then peel or gently scrape off. If it still won't budge, aim a hair dryer, set on low, at the item for half a minute. The heat will loosen the glue.

Upholding upholstery

Gillette shaving cream makes an excellent upholstery cleaner in a pinch. It sticks to all the tricky parts, like the backs of chairs or the chair legs. Just spray on a small amount and work it into the fabric with your fingers or a soft brush. Sponge off the excess and blot the area to encourage drying.

Make your own upholstery cleaner: Mix ¼ cup Dawn Dishwashing Detergent and 1 cup warm water. Use an eggbeater to whip the mixture into a foam. Apply the foam using an upholstery brush with stiff bristles and working in one small area at a time. Remove excess with a damp O-Cel-O sponge. Do not oversaturate.

Polish vinyl or plastic furniture by applying Simoniz Original Paste Wax. Use a small amount, then buff to shine.

Remove water spots or other marks from vinyl furniture by rubbing them with Pepsodent toothpaste on a damp cloth.

A spot of spilled glue on furniture can be removed by applying vegetable oil to the area and rubbing until the sticky stuff is removed.

White rings or spots can be removed from leather furniture by applying a bit of Vaseline Petroleum Jelly to the area and leaving it on for 24 to 48 hours. Remove the Vaseline with a soft cloth, then buff.

Glorious glass surfaces

Final Touch fabric softener cleans glass surfaces without adding lint. Mix 1 capful with 1 gallon warm water. Use an O-Cel-O sponge to wipe a glass or Plexiglas surface clean.

Magnificent marble

Chalk cleans polished marble and metal surfaces. Crush Crayola Chalk in a GLAD Zipper Bag, tapping it gently with a hammer. Dip a soft cloth into the powder and rub the surface.

Marble countertops can be cleaned with a moist cloth dipped in 20 Mule Team Borax. Rub the surface, then rinse with warm water.

Remove a stain on a marble surface by mixing equal parts ammonia and hydrogen peroxide. Apply with a soft cloth. Let dry, then rub with a dry cloth. Wipe again with a dampened cloth.

ALL-PURPOSE CLEANER

Borax and Dawn Dishwashing Detergent are the key ingredients to this all-purpose cleaner you can make yourself.

Recipe Box

1 teaspoon 20 Mule Team Borax
1 teaspoon baking soda
2 teaspoons white vinegar
¼ teaspoon Dawn Dishwashing Detergent
2 cups hot water

Mix ingredients together, then pour into a clean, empty spray bottle and store with your other cleaning supplies.

Electrasol Automatic Dishwashing detergent is another great all-purpose cleaner. Just dissolve ¼ cup Electrasol in 1 gallon very hot water, then scrub surfaces with an O-Cel-O sponge. Be sure to wear rubber gloves.

Brassy brass

Brass fixtures in your home can be kept from tarnishing if you rub them with Simoniz Original Paste Wax after you clean them.

Spray Pledge furniture polish onto a piece of very fine steel wool. This can safely clean brass items.

A mixture of salt and Pepsodent toothpaste can clean tarnished brass items.

If you use brass serving dishes for your fancy meals, rub them with a little olive oil after you've cleaned them. This will prevent tarnishing.

Mix flour with salt and add 1 teaspoon white vinegar so the ingredients form a paste. Apply in a thick layer to brass and wait for it to dry to the touch. Rinse with water, then wipe off the paste.

When lacquer is lacking

Black lacquered figurines or other decorative pieces can be washed in a solution of strong brewed tea. Wipe with a soft cloth.

To polish lacquered metal items, rub the item with a few drops of olive oil on a soft cloth.

When soot doesn't suit you

Clean the grime and soot from fireplace tools or andirons by dipping a steel wool ball (grade 000) into vegetable oil and rubbing the dirty items. Then apply a polish.

When cleaning your fireplace, sprinkle damp coffee grounds over the cooled ashes to keep down the dust.

Wax on, wax off
Keep melted wax from building up in your candleholders: Coat the inside of the holders with Vaseline Petroleum Jelly before inserting candles.

Wood trinkets
 Clean and shine wooden knickknacks and other wood objects in your home by coating them with a thin layer of Alberto VO5 Conditioning Hairdressing. Buff to a shine.

Vases
Clean stains in a flower vase by dropping 2 Alka-Seltzer tablets in the vase with water. Let sit, swish liquid around, and rinse.

Polident Denture Cleanser tablets can be used to clean the gunk out of vases. Fill the vase with water and add 1 Polident tablet. Let soak; rinse.

OH, WHAT AN ODOR!
Surprising air fresheners
A little vanilla extract on a cotton ball can make a quick and easy air freshener. Store these in bathroom or kitchen wastebaskets or any place where nasty odors linger.

Make your own air freshener by brewing up
1 quart tea, adding 4 teaspoons lemon juice, and
pouring into a spray bottle. Lightly squirt the
mixture wherever odors are a problem.

Clean-smelling clothes
Add Downy Sheets to linen drawers and closets
to help keep fabrics smelling fresh.

Eliminate mildew odors in drawers
and other items by wiping the surface
with full-strength Scope mouthwash.

Out with the trash
 Line the bottom of your kitchen
garbage can with 1 inch Fresh Step
cat litter to help absorb grease and to
control moisture and odors.

Place a Downy Sheet at the bottom of your
household's wastebaskets to help control odors.

It must be musty
 Add Downy Sheets to closed suitcases, backpacks, trunks, and purses
that might be stored for long periods
of time. The sheets will help reduce
musty, stale smells.

Add 4 teaspoons lemon juice to the water in your humidifier to eliminate stale odors.

If you own a summer lake cabin or other building that will be shut up for a long period of time, control damp, musty odors while you're gone by filling shallow boxes with Fresh Step cat litter and storing one in each room of the house.

A Downy Sheet can control odor and musty smells under your kitchen or bathroom sinks or under any sink area that is damp.

You can dry out the moisture in a damp book by sprinkling the pages with cornstarch and letting it sit overnight. Then brush the cornstarch out.

Tuck Downy Sheets under your chair or couch cushions to help freshen furniture. This is especially helpful if you have a dog that is allowed onto your furniture.

PROTECTING PERSONAL ITEMS
Sparkle and shine jewelry
Any jewelry with diamonds, sapphires, rubies, or emeralds can be made to sparkle again by soaking them in club soda.

Dissolve 2 Alka-Seltzer tablets in a glass of water and use this to soak dull or tarnished jewelry. Let soak for only 2 minutes, then rub dry.

Use Polident Denture Cleanser tablets dissolved in a glass of water to make your diamonds sparkle. Just drop in the jewelry for 2 minutes.

To prevent silver or costume jewelry from tarnishing, place a piece of Crayola Chalk in the jewelry box.

Olive or vegetable oil makes a good cleaner for pearls. Just dab a little on each pearl, then wipe dry with a soft cloth.

Put a little Pepsodent toothpaste on your fingertips, then use it to rub silver jewelry. Let the toothpaste sit about 1 hour or more. Rub off with a soft cloth.

JEWELRY CLEANER

Make your own basic jewelry cleaner: Combine ¼ cup ammonia, ¼ cup Dawn Dishwashing Detergent, and ¾ cup water. Mix well. Soak the jewelry for 5 minutes. Clean around ridges with a soft toothbrush. Buff dry. (Do not use this on plastics, gold-plated jewelry, or soft stones such as opals, pearls, or jade.)

Chapter 4

The clothes
Hamper

How many times have you reached for a specialty product in your laundry only to find the bottle empty? When that happens, there are plenty of substitutes—products that will work just as well or better and sometimes cost a lot less, too. Try some of these solutions to clean, patch, remove stains, and make clothes last longer. You may decide not to go back to the high-priced products at all!

THE LAUNDRY LIFE
Washing machine worries

To kill germs inside a washing machine, add ½ cup Scope mouthwash to the wash water. You can also use Scope to kill germs on the outside of the machine.

If you accidentally put too much soap in your washing machine, kill the suds by adding a capful of Final Touch fabric softener to the load.

Handle with care

Here's a handy tip from a professional launderer: Use Ivory liquid soap instead of those expensive products that say "for fine washables." Ivory is gentle and cleans just as well.

White the right way

White polyester fabric will look even whiter if you soak it overnight in a mixture of ½ cup Electrasol Automatic Dishwashing Detergent and 1 gallon warm water. Launder as usual, but add ½ cup vinegar to the final rinse.

For a super whitening mix, dissolve ½ cup Electrasol Automatic Dishwashing Detergent in 1 gallon warm water and add ½ cup Clorox Bleach. Soak whites for 1 to 8 hours (the longer the better), then launder as usual.

Keep white nylon curtains white by soaking them in a solution of ½ cup baking soda in 1 gallon water.

You can also whiten yellowed linens by dropping 1 or 2 Polident Denture Cleanser tablets in a tub of warm water and soaking the fabrics overnight.

Bleach soiled handkerchiefs by soaking them for a few hours in a solution of warm water and 1 tablespoon cream of tartar.

To clean white kid gloves, rub Johnson's Baby Powder into them. Let sit for a few minutes, then brush off the powder.

Brighten up
To brighten colored clothes that can't tolerate chlorine bleach, add ½ cup baking soda or ½ cup 20 Mule Team Borax to your wash along with your detergent. Then add ½ cup vinegar to the final rinse.

Oh so soft
Out of fabric softener? You can add 1 or 2 capfuls of Suave hair conditioner to your laundry's final rinse to make clothes softer and eliminate static.

Don't give me static
To remove static cling from clothes, slightly dampen a Downy Sheet and rub it over clothes.

A Ringing Solution

Remove ring-around-the-collar with one of these methods:
- Rub Crayola Chalk into the collar, then wash as usual.
- Pour Suave shampoo along the collar and allow it to soak into the ring. Let it sit—the longer the better—then wash.
- The grease-cutting agents in Dawn Dishwashing Detergent can help remove ring-around-the-collar. Paint on, let sit, then launder.

 Make your own fabric softener sheets by sprinkling Final Touch fabric softener on a Scott Towel, an O-Cel-O sponge, or a clean cloth and tossing it in the dryer.

Massage Vaseline Intensive Care lotion into your hands, then pass your hands over static-prone clothes.

Tips to dye for
If you just can't get those dingy whites clean, don't discard them. Dye them off-white or darker in a batch of strong tea, rinsing in cold water. Repeat until desired shade is achieved.

To dye fabrics brown, soak them in a bath of strong instant coffee. Repeat until dark enough.

Light spots on black suede can be covered up with a strong solution of instant coffee.

CURES FOR PANTY HOSE WOES

If you give your panty hose an occasional bath in a mixture of ½ cup salt to 1 quart of water, they'll last longer.

Another life extender for panty hose is to add some Final Touch fabric softener to the final rinse when washing them.

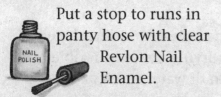

Put a stop to runs in panty hose with clear Revlon Nail Enamel.

Another fix for runs in panty hose is to spray the area with Finesse Hair Spray; let dry before wearing.

SOCK IT TO DAMP STOCKINGS

In a hurry to get to work? Dry just-washed panty hose in a jiffy with a hair dryer set on low.

Slick fabric suggestions

Give the sheer curtains in your home a permanent-press-like finish. Just add a packet of plain gelatin to hot water and pour into the washing machine's final rinse.

If your new jeans are too stiff, soak them overnight in a tub of water with a capful of Final Touch fabric softener. Rinse in clean water before drying.

 To condition leather, rub some Alberto VO5 Conditioning Hairdressing into it.

CLOTHESPIN CARRIER

Make a clothespin holder by cutting a hole opposite the handle in a clean, dry Clorox Bleach bottle. Hang from the handle on your clothesline and toss clothespins in.

You can reclaim a chamois that has hardened from being wet and drying out. Add 1 tablespoon vegetable oil to a pan of water and soak the chamois in it.

 To put body back in your permanent-press clothes, dissolve powdered milk in some water and add to the final rinse of your washing machine.

Grease is the word

Pour cola or club soda directly on a greasy spot. Let it sit for a few minutes to loosen the stain, then wash as usual.

To cut grease on really dirty clothes, pour a can of cola into the wash along with your usual detergent.

Loosen up grease spots on clothes by rubbing them with Crayola Chalk before washing.

For fresh grease spills on fabric, cover them with cornmeal and allow it to absorb as much as possible. Brush off and launder.

Greasy spots on suede can be removed by blotting the area with a cloth dipped in vinegar. Dry the fabric, then brush to bring back the nap.

GREASE STAIN ATTACK

Grease stains can sometimes be removed by rubbing Johnson's Baby Powder or cornstarch into them. Allow the powder to sit for an hour or more to soak up the grease, then brush off and wash as usual. If stains remain, repeat until they're gone.

Other super stain solutions

Pretreat tough stains before washing by sprinkling Electrasol Automatic Dishwashing Detergent on the spot and scrubbing with an old toothbrush dipped in water.

To remove ink stains, spray Finesse Hair Spray on the spot, and blot with a Scott Towel. Continue spraying and blotting until ink is gone.

Squeeze a bit of Pepsodent toothpaste on ink stains and then scrub with a brush. Rinse with clean water.

Try removing rust stains from clothes by adding 1 cup lemon juice to the load along with the usual detergent.

For blood stains, mix a paste of cornstarch and water and apply to the stain right away. Let dry, then brush off. Repeat if necessary.

If blood leaves a stain, try cleaning with 3 percent Rite Aid hydrogen peroxide. Test a hidden area first to be sure the fabric is colorfast. Dab on the peroxide, then blot off, repeating as necessary.

For tough stains on baby clothes, soak the items (colorfast only) in a bucket of water with ¼ cup Clorox Bleach added. Wait 10 minutes, rinse in clean water, then launder as usual.

If you get spots on white suede, cover them with Crayola Chalk.

Club soda, either straight from the bottle or flat, is a great emergency cleaner for clothes. Apply it with a damp cloth.

To remove tough juice stains, mix ⅓ cup vinegar or lemon juice with water. Soak the stain in this solution, then wash as usual.

To remove mildew from clothes, soak the item in a solution of 1 cup vinegar to 1 gallon water. If mildew persists, repeat, adding more vinegar.

Loosen lipstick stains from clothing by rubbing Vaseline Petroleum Jelly into the stain before laundering.

For tough stains, make a paste of lemon juice and salt. Apply to the stain, set the item in the sun to dry, then wash as usual.

Perspiration stains can sometimes be removed by soaking the clothes in salt water. Dissolve ¼ cup salt in a tub of water, soak overnight, then wash.

Those hard-to-fix bleach spots might be fixable with a Crayola Crayon. Pick a matching color, warm the fabric with an iron, and color the spot. Cover it with Reynolds Cut-Rite Wax Paper and iron on low to set the color.

STAIN REMOVER

¼ cup vinegar
¼ cup ammonia
2 tablespoons baking soda
1 tablespoon Ivory liquid soap
1 quart water

Mix ingredients well, and put in spray bottle. Spray on stains and let sit for a few minutes before washing.

Another bleach-spot fix is to mix food coloring until you have the right shade, paint on, and let dry.

When baby spits up on you, grab a Pampers baby wipe to clean up the mess.

PRESSING MATTERS

Cut your ironing time by putting a piece of Reynolds Wrap Aluminum Foil under the ironing board cover. The foil will reflect heat so you're actually ironing from both sides at once.

To remove built-up starch from an iron, pass it over a piece of Reynolds Wrap Aluminum Foil.

Remove cleaning-product residues from the vents of an electric iron (cool only) with a Q-Tip Cotton Swab. For tough deposits, first dip the swab in Rite Aid rubbing alcohol.

SWELL SMELL QUELLERS

To get rid of odors in sneakers, fill socks or the ends of No nonsense panty hose legs with Fresh Step cat litter. Close the ends of the socks or panty hose legs with rubber bands, and stuff into sneakers whenever you're not wearing them.

STIFF COMPETITION

You can make your own spray starch by dissolving 1 tablespoon cornstarch in 2 cups water. Use a clean spray bottle to dispense. For a heavier starch, use 2 or more tablespoons cornstarch.

A Downy Sheet, bunched up and placed in sneakers, will help deodorize them.

To cover odors from dirty laundry, keep a Downy Sheet in the bottom of your laundry basket, bag, or hamper.

SO INTO SEWING
On the mend

If your vinyl, leather, or soft luggage develops a tear while you're on the road, repair it with Reach Dental Floss and a sturdy needle. Floss is strong and won't stick to the fabric.

When the down in a jacket gets flattened and compacted, fluff it up by tumbling the jacket in the dryer with a couple of Penn tennis balls.

Keep buckles from chipping or tarnishing by painting them with clear Revlon Nail Enamel. This also helps keep buckles shiny.

Small ribbons on garments that keep coming untied can be fixed in place by putting a dab of clear Revlon Nail Enamel over the knot.

When you buy a new garment, dab the center of each button with clear Revlon Nail Enamel to seal the threads. The buttons will stay on longer.

To loosen a sticky zipper, rub Blistex Lip Balm up and down the length of it. Open and close the zipper a few times to distribute the lubricant.

Alberto VO5 Conditioning Hairdressing also works to fix troublesome zippers. Rub it on and work the zipper a few times.

Paint the edges of fraying garments with clear Revlon Nail Enamel.

Sew good ideas

To fasten buttons more securely, sew them on with Reach Dental Floss instead of thread. Just color the floss with a matching Crayola Marker or Crayola Crayon.

Use an Elmer's Glue Stick instead of pins and/or basting when making lapped seams. Apply the glue to the underside of the overlapping section. Press in place, let dry 1 or 2 minutes, and topstitch.

To make needle-threading easier, stick the end of the thread into Revlon Nail Enamel and allow to dry. Red polish will make the thread easier to see and will provide a slick end for threading.

You can temporarily hold nonfusible interfacing in place with adhesive from an Elmer's Glue Stick. This eliminates the need to baste interfacing to the garment piece.

GOOD NEWS FOR SHOES

Neaten up the frayed ends of shoelaces (and make it easier to lace them) by dipping them in clear Revlon Nail Enamel.

You can use Vaseline Petroleum Jelly to shine leather shoes. Apply with a soft cloth, wipe off the excess, and buff.

Out on the road with no shoe polish? Try using Blistex Lip Balm. Rub it over your shoes and polish with a soft cloth.

Spray Pledge furniture polish on shoes, then buff with a clean, dry cloth.

Spray Niagara spray starch on new fabric tennis shoes before wearing them—dirt can't become embedded in the canvas, and the shoes will always be easy to clean.

Use lemon juice to clean and shine black or tan leathers. Apply with a soft cloth.

Melitta coffee filters make great applicators for shoe polish and are good for shining, too.

In a hurry? A Pampers baby wipe will give your shoes a quick shine as you're heading out the door.

To take scuff marks off shoes, rub a bit of Pepsodent toothpaste onto the marks and wipe off with a clean cloth.

To keep shoes shiny after you've polished them, give them a spray with Finesse Hair Spray to protect and seal the shine.

Winter can be tough on shoes. To protect them, coat them with a thin layer of Alberto VO5 Conditioning Hairdressing.

Alberto VO5 Conditioning Hairdressing can also help if your shoes tend to squeak.

Vaseline Intensive Care lotion can be used to shine shoes. Just put a little on each shoe, rub in with your fingers, and buff until dry.

Chapter 5

The Chef's Pantry

Any cook worth her salt in the kitchen knows there's more than one way to do just about anything. If you're out of one ingredient—substitute! If something flops—fake it! You may have been baking grandma's recipe for 20 years, but that's no reason you can't spice it up a little. Here are some tips and tricks on unusual ways you can substitute, preserve, prepare, and be cool in the kitchen.

MEAT MATTERS
Marinades the easy way

It's easiest to marinate meats not in a bowl or pan but in a GLAD Zipper Bag. The bag allows for full coverage, and you can easily flip the bag at intervals to make sure the marinade reaches all parts of the meat.

Marinate any cut of meat in beer for 1 hour. The beer adds an interesting flavor and tenderizes as well as any other marinade.

Try a little tenderness

Drop a wine cork into a pot of stew to help tenderize the meat. Be sure to remove the cork before serving!

Tenderize a pot roast or stew meat by marinating it in equal parts strong brewed tea and double-strength beef broth.

 Before wrapping your meat for the freezer, brush it with a little olive oil to prevent it from drying out.

Prime poultry

You can strain poultry or beef broth through a Melitta coffee filter to help strain out some of the fat that has accumulated on the top.

To make skinning chicken parts easier, grab the chicken in one hand with a Melitta basket coffee filter. The filter will give you some traction on the slippery skin, and then you can throw the filter away.

When roasting a turkey, tie its legs together with Reach Dental Floss.

Fishy business
Return a frozen fish to its original fresh taste. When thawing, cover it with a mixture of ¾ cup water and 1⅓ cups dry milk.

You can cover unskinned fish with a layer of whipped cream to get rid of the odor.

DAIRY DELIGHTS
Cheese, please!
Hard cheeses that are difficult to cut can be tamed by cutting through them with unflavored Reach Dental Floss.

 When grating cheese, spray your grater with Pam cooking spray to make it slide better and make cleaning up easier.

Prevent hard cheeses from drying out by adding a few drops of vinegar to a moist Scott Towel. Wrap the cheese in the paper towel and put it inside a GLAD Zipper Bag. If the paper towel dries out, add more water or vinegar.

Shredded mozzarella or other types of cheese typically used on pizza will keep longer in the freezer. Store the cheese in its original bag, but put the bag inside a GLAD Zipper Bag.

LOSE THE FAT

Here's a low-fat tip: Use whipped cream as a substitute for cream in coffee.

Did you know the handiest low-fat cheese spread is yogurt? Put plain, nonfat yogurt in a Melitta cone coffee filter, cover the filter with GLAD Cling Wrap, and let it drain overnight in the refrigerator. You can then flavor the yogurt cheese with any herb of choice and use it as a cracker or sandwich spread.

It's just a yoke

Use a Q-Tip Cotton Swab to remove any yolk that may have gotten into your egg whites. This is especially important when making a meringue.

SAUCE AND SUCH

To give an interesting flavor to traditional spaghetti sauce, add ¼ teaspoon instant coffee to the pot. The coffee tones down the acidic flavor a bit and darkens the sauce.

A quick, interesting glaze for baked ham is a can of cola. Pour it onto the ham, then wrap the meat with Reynolds Wrap Aluminum Foil. A half hour before the ham is done, remove the foil. The drippings will make an excellent gravy.

When cooking a stew or sauce with herbs, first marinate the herbs in 2 tablespoons olive oil for 30 minutes. Marinating brings out the herb flavors.

GET MOVIN'!

When a new bottle of ketchup just won't get started, insert a GLAD flexible straw into the bottle to add air and get the ketchup flowing.

Use up leftover cranberry sauce (say, after Thanksgiving) by making a meatball sauce from 1 can of cranberries and 4 ounces tomato sauce.

You can reuse oil from frying if you strain it first. Run it through a sieve lined with a Melitta coffee filter.

Dressing sits better on dry salad greens. To dry yours in a pinch, aim a hair dryer set on the lowest setting at the leaves.

SWEET TREATS
Let them eat cake!

 Cutting 1 layer of a layer cake into yet another thin layer can be tricky, but you can do it with unflavored Reach Dental Floss. First, insert toothpicks horizontally into the cake at the cutting line. Then, holding a long length of dental floss tightly between your hands, start at the far side and pull the floss toward you, using the toothpicks as a guide.

EASY ICING

To make an easy cake-icing tool, put the icing in a quart-size GLAD Zipper Bag. Squeeze the bag to make the icing go to one corner, then snip off a small piece of the corner. Twist and carefully squeeze the bag to make the icing come out. With practice, you'll be able to make designs and write names. (This trick works for whipped cream, too.)

Line an 8-inch round cake pan with a flattened Melitta basket coffee filter to keep the cake from sticking to the pan.

When making a chocolate cake from a box, don't use plain water. Instead, add a teaspoon of instant coffee to the water and you'll have mocha cake!

SNOWFLAKE YOUR CAKE

Use a Melitta coffee filter to make a fancy stencil for powdering the tops of cakes or pastries. Fold the filter in half, then in half again, and snip a design into it—much like you would to make paper snowflakes. Apply a light coat of Pam cooking spray to the filter, set it on top of the cake, and sprinkle powdered sugar over it.

When you need to cover an iced cake or cupcakes with plastic wrap, spray the wrap first with Pam cooking spray and the icing won't stick to it.

Marshmallow mayhem

Instead of pushing birthday candles directly into a cake, set them into marshmallows, then set the marshmallows on the cake. This adds a decorative touch, and if the candles drip too much, just toss out the marshmallows.

Before filling a sugar cone with ice cream, add a drip prevention method: Drop in a marshmallow.

CHOCOLATE TREAT

Pour chocolate milk into a 5-ounce waxed Dixie cup, stick in a wooden craft stick, and freeze it for a fudge-pop treat.

NOT JUST WHISTLING DIXIE CUPS

Here's a basic gingerbread recipe with kid-size pans and kid-friendly instructions. It requires an adult cook, however.

In 1 Dixie cup, add 3 tablespoons packaged gingerbread mix to 1 tablespoon water. Mix until moistened. Bake this in an electric skillet set at 400°F. (Really. It won't burn!)

For a more advanced recipe, mix the gingerbread as directed above. In another Dixie cup, add 1 teaspoon salad oil, sprinkle 1 teaspoon brown sugar over the oil, then carefully add 1 tablespoon crushed, drained canned pineapple on top of the sugar. Pour your cup of gingerbread mix over the top, and bake as directed above.

Recipe Box

Marshmallows make excellent quick frosting for cupcakes. When baking cupcakes, add a marshmallow to the top of each one about 1 minute before they're done baking. The marshmallows will melt into instant frosting!

Line your pie shell with a layer of marshmallows before adding canned pumpkin filling. The marshmallows rise to the top during the baking process and give the pie an instant sweet, sticky topping.

NO-FREEZE ICE CREAM

You don't need a fancy automatic ice cream machine or an old-fashioned freezer to make ice cream in a hurry at home.

½ cup milk (whole, 2 percent, chocolate, or fat free)
1 tablespoon sugar
¼ teaspoon vanilla (or other flavoring)

Combine all ingredients in a small GLAD Zipper Bag. Zip the bag shut, then place it inside a quart-size or larger GLAD Zipper Bag. Add enough ice to the outer bag to fill it halfway, then put in 6 tablespoons salt. Zip the larger bag shut. Now take turns tossing and turning, shaking and mixing the 2 bags in your hands. (It gets cold. You may want to hold a dishtowel while you do this if you don't have helpers.) After about 5 or 10 minutes of shaking, the mixture will be the consistency of ice cream. Note: The ingredient amounts listed do not make very much ice cream, but don't double the recipe. If you need more, make several small batches.

Cookie time

Cookies lift off a cookie sheet easily if you run a piece of Reach Dental Floss underneath them.

Add a little food coloring to gelatin powder and sprinkle fresh-baked cookies with the colored powder.

Jam on

If you seem to have a whole bunch of open jelly and jam jars, use them to make your own flavored syrups. Mix 1 cup corn syrup with 4 tablespoons jam or preserves, and stir over low heat. Store in the refrigerator.

Want cheese with that?

Mix gelatin with 1 cup boiling water, then add 1 cup red wine for an interesting twist on dessert. Refrigerate at least 4 hours.

PERFECTLY PRESERVED

Prolong the life of lettuce in your crisper drawer by wrapping it in a Scott Towel first, then in a GLAD Zipper Bag.

A pinch of salt can help a carton of milk last longer in the refrigerator. Add the pinch when you first open the carton.

Cut fruit will stay fresh in the refrigerator without turning brown if you coat the fruit with lemon juice.

SIMPLE SUBSTITUTIONS

Use club soda in place of the liquid in your pancake recipe and pancakes will fluff up.

Packaged whipped cream with a little lemon juice added can become sour cream in a pinch. Let it sit for 30 minutes, then serve.

Here's an easy way to make low-fat whipped cream: Beat 1 cup dry milk in 1 cup ice water for about 5 minutes. Serve immediately.

Stir 1 tablespoon molasses into 1 cup sugar and use in place of brown sugar if you're out. For dark brown sugar, add 2 tablespoons molasses.

KEEP IT CLEAN
Dough to dough
When you begin a dough-kneading project or some other messy, hands-on task in the kitchen, keep an open GLAD Zipper Bag near your telephone. You'll be able to pick up the phone even with messy hands by just slipping your hand in the bag.

Spray your spatulas, spoons, and mixing bowls with Pam cooking spray when tackling a pastry-making project. This will keep things moving quicker and make cleanup easier.

Knead and roll out dough for a pie right inside a GLAD Zipper Bag to create less mess.

Before a stain becomes a stain

Keep a small container of Johnson's Baby Powder in your kitchen cupboard and use it to immediately attack grease stains on your clothing. Sprinkle the powder onto the splatter and rub to absorb the grease.

After working with berries or other fruit that stains, rinse your hands with lemon juice to get rid of the color.

Funnel through

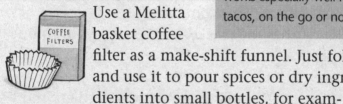

Use a Melitta basket coffee filter as a make-shift funnel. Just fold and use it to pour spices or dry ingredients into small bottles, for example. Or cut off the tip of a cone-type filter.

Shape a piece of Reynolds Wrap Aluminum Foil into a cone and use it as a funnel.

FOOD ON THE GO

If you're dashing out the door with something edible yet messy, wrap it in a Melitta basket coffee filter to avoid drips. This trick works especially well for tacos, on the go or no.

What a drip

Spread a sheet of Reynolds Wrap Aluminum Foil on the oven rack below a baking pan if you fear boilovers and spills. Don't spread the foil on the bottom of an oven.

Weigh down

Before putting messy foods on a kitchen scale to weigh them, put them in a Melitta basket coffee filter and keep your scale clean.

If I had a hammer

When you need cracker crumbs for a recipe, put your crackers in a GLAD Zipper Bag and roll a rolling pin over them. This contains the mess, crushes the crackers, and keeps your rolling pin clean.

Similarly, when you need ground peppercorns or other whole spices crushed, place them in a small GLAD Zipper Bag, and use a meat tenderizing hammer or even your rolling pin to smash them.

Pan prep

Apply a layer of vegetable oil to rust spots on your cast-iron skillet. Let stand overnight, then wipe the pan thoroughly. Rust should disappear.

After seasoning a cast-iron skillet with a drop of vegetable oil, store it between 2 Melitta basket coffee filters to help keep moisture at bay.

COOKING WOES

Alleviate sticky rice by cooking it in water with 2 tablespoons vinegar. The vinegar will add a slightly tangy taste. You can also substitute lemon juice for the vinegar.

If a piece of cork breaks off into your fine wine while opening it, pour the wine into a glass through a Melitta coffee filter. Just stretch the filter tightly over the wine bottle.

TIPS FOR TOOLS
Not measuring up?

If you can't see the marks on your measuring cup—either they're faded or your eyes aren't what they used to be—remake the markings by applying red Revlon Nail Enamel to the marks.

Add a quick spray of Pam cooking spray to the lip of a measuring cup or pitcher to prevent dribbling.

Catch the wave

An easy way to avoid splatters in the microwave is to cover open bowls and dishes with a Melitta basket coffee filter.

There's nothing magic about instant oatmeal. In a microwave, you can cook regular oatmeal just as fast, then customize it with your own spices and fruits.

Get the scoop

Cut out the bottom of a clean Clorox Bleach bottle, then shape the bottle into a triangle to form a scooper. Use for pet food or bulk supplies of rice, sugar, or flour.

Chapter 6

Family Fun and Household Projects

If you're a crafty person, you already know how easy it is to turn common objects and food products into works of art at home. The following tips can help even the least crafty person create something fun as a rainy day project with children or a special home-made gift for the holidays. Take a look around your house. We bet you'll find plenty of ideas!

CRAFT FAIR BOUND
Wood you, could you?

When working on small woodworking crafts, you can hide a scratch or touch up a smudge by mixing 1 teaspoon instant coffee crystals with 2 teaspoons water. Use a Q-Tip Cotton Swab to apply the liquid to the mark.

Make nails, screws, and brads go into wood easier by first stabbing them into Ivory bar soap to lubricate them.

Crafty cleanup

If you've just stained your hands and fingernails with craft paint, wash and scrub with baking soda. Dig your fingernails right into the soda, too.

Sew it on

Sewing a craft project becomes easier if you wipe your needle and thread with a Downy Sheet.

Dip the end of thread in clear Revlon Nail Enamel to help thread it through a needle.

APPLYING APPLIQUÉS

When planning an appliqué project, create a template by drawing your design on a piece of Reynolds Freezer Paper. Draw on the dull side, then pin the paper to the wrong side of the appliqué fabric, keeping the shiny side of the paper against the fabric. Cut the fabric ¼ inch beyond the paper. Fold the fabric edge over the freezer paper, and press the fabric with a hot iron to tack it. Sew the appliqué onto the fabric used for your project, then, before you finish stitching, pull out the freezer paper through a small hole.

T-Shirt Stencils

Use the dull side of Reynolds Freezer Paper to draw a stencil design. Cut out the design, then iron the paper stencil onto a t-shirt, keeping the shiny side against the fabric. With the stencil attached to the t-shirt, put a second piece of freezer paper behind the stencil (inside the shirt) to soak up any excess paint. Paint the design using fabric paint. Remove the freezer paper after the garment cools.

When removing stitches from black or very dark fabric, run a line of Crayola Chalk around the stitch path. This will make it much easier to see when you resew the fabric. The chalk will wash right out.

Craft clutter

When you've used up your Pampers baby wipes, keep the plastic containers. They are perfect for storing all the odds and ends of craft projects, such as string, ribbon, glue sticks, beads, and so on. Then use a Crayola Marker to label the container for easy identification.

When you need to stop a painting project midstream, instead of washing out your brush, tightly seal it with Reynolds Wrap Aluminum Foil or in a GLAD Zipper Bag. The paint won't dry out before you return.

STAY SHARP

Sharpen your craft scissors by cutting a piece of Reynolds Wrap Aluminum Foil several times.

A garden that keeps on giving

Collect dried flowers and pinecones and store them in a GLAD Zipper Bag. Add bay leaves, cloves, a cinnamon stick, and a few drops of cinnamon oil. Keep the bag sealed a few weeks, then add the potpourri to decorative dishes throughout your house.

Dry out and preserve your last bouquet from the garden. First find a box to hold the flowers, then mix 3 parts 20 Mule Team Borax with 10 parts cornmeal. Cover the flowers completely and let them sit 2 weeks.

Flowers can be dried by pressing them between 2 Scott Towels stuck between the pages of a telephone book.

Spritz a little Finesse Hair Spray on delicate greenery or baby's breath to keep it looking fresh longer. Don't saturate.

HANDY HOME PROJECT HINTS
Crack up
A crack in a piece of china or a commemorative plate will eventually attract dirt and dust. Place the plate in a large saucepan filled with 1⅓ cups dry milk and 3¾ cups water (make sure your china is heat resistant). Boil the mixture, then let it simmer 45 minutes.

Candle cleanup
Shine and dust candles by wiping them with a cloth sprayed with Pledge furniture polish.

Valuable protection
Use Melitta coffee filters between stored china or delicate pieces to protect them.

ATTRACTIVE AIR FRESHENER

In a medium saucepan, mix 4 packages gelatin with 1 cup near-boiling distilled water; stir to dissolve. Remove from heat and add another cup of water. If desired, add 10 drops scented essential oil and food coloring. Pour mixture into clean baby food jars, and let sit overnight. Add the cap if giving the air freshener as a gift, or place around your home for a fresh scent.

Scrapbook Know-How

You can prevent your valued newspaper clippings from turning yellow. Dissolve 1 Phillips' Milk of Magnesia tablet in 1 quart club soda and let the solution sit overnight. Stir well, then pour the mixture into a shallow pan and soak your clippings in it for 1 hour. Blot the clippings between Scott Towels, then spread on a window screen to dry.

Wallpaper woes

To help remove old wallpaper, mix a capful of Final Touch fabric softener in 1 quart hot water. Sponge this on the wallpaper, let sit 20 minutes, then peel off.

Add a few drops of food coloring to your wallpaper paste during a wall-papering project. This will help you easily see how well—or not so well— you are spreading the paste.

Kid Craftiness
Craft cover-up

When children are working on crafts, line their work surface with Reynolds Freezer Paper to prevent paint and glue stains.

Place paint or glue bottles on the craft table inside a hole cut into an O-Cel-O sponge. The sponge will prevent tipping and will soak up any drips.

Sticky situations
Make your own colorful glues by using Elmer's glue and adding a few drops of food coloring.

For cement glue spills on furniture, rub the dried glue with peanut butter.

SALT KID'S DOUGH

1 cup flour
½ cup salt
2 tablespoons cream of tartar
1 cup water
1 tablespoon vegetable oil

Make your own sculpting clay at home. Mix flour, salt, and cream of tartar in a medium saucepan. Add water and oil. Cook over medium heat for 3 to 5 minutes or until the mixture becomes the consistency of dough. Let cool, then add a few drops of food coloring if desired. Store in an airtight container or a GLAD Zipper Bag.

Glue in a pinch: Mix flour and water to a slightly thick liquid and use this to glue cardboard, paper, and fabrics.

If you can't bead 'em...

Use Reach Waxed Dental Floss to string beads.

Cut GLAD flexible straws into ½-inch sections and string the pieces with Reach Dental Floss to make colorful necklaces.

Projects in a pinch

Simulate a lava lamp by filling a glass with club soda and raisins. The raisins float up and down with the carbonation. Even better, add food coloring and pour the liquid into a decorative bottle.

Give an older child a chance to take up sculpting. Have him or her carve figurines using Ivory bar soap and a dull table knife.

CALL IT MACARONI

Fill small bowls with water and a few drops food coloring. Drop macaroni noodles into the water until they change color, then remove, drain, and dry the noodles on a Scott Towel. String them on Reach Dental Floss to make a colorful necklace.

Give each child a square of Reynolds Freezer Paper to decorate as his or her very own place mat.

Have the child dip a Q-Tip Cotton Swab in lemon juice and write or draw on plain white paper. To make the design appear, hold the paper near a hot lightbulb. (Supervise children as they do this.)

HOLIDAY HEYDAY
Costume craze

Add glitter to your face by rubbing a little Vaseline Petroleum Jelly on your cheeks and sprinkling on glitter. Be careful not to get glitter in your eyes.

If you want sparkling hair, comb a little Vaseline Petroleum Jelly through your hair and sprinkle with glitter. This also works if you need a dusting of gray in your hair: After applying Vaseline, sprinkle on Johnson's Baby Powder.

To make a white clown or ghost face, mix 2 tablespoons cornstarch with 1 tablespoon vegetable shortening. If color is needed, use drops of food coloring. Apply mixture to face.

Fake a scar: Add 1 packet gelatin to hot water, and when it cools enough, draw a strip of it across your face. As it dries further, it will appear to be a scar.

Pumpkin preservation

The cut, exposed edges of your carved pumpkin will last longer in cold weather if you coat the edges with Vaseline Petroleum Jelly.

CHRISTMAS CLAY ORNAMENTS

Mix ½ cup salt and ½ cup water in a pan and bring to a boil. Meanwhile, place ½ cup cold water in a small bowl and stir in ½ cup cornstarch. Add a few drops food coloring to the cornstarch mixture. Add the cornstarch mixture to the boiling salt water, stirring continually until the mixture is stiff. Remove from heat, and cool slightly. Turn the mixture onto a cutting board. Let cool, and knead until it is the consistency of clay. Store in an airtight container or a GLAD Zipper Bag if you are not going to use immediately.

To make Christmas decorations, roll out the dough and cut with cookie cutters or shape freehand. Use a toothpick or drinking straw to make a hole in the top for hanging. Bake at 200°F for 2 hours. Decorate and hang with string or twist ties.

Giant Chocolate Kiss

When the gift you bought presents a wrapping challenge, center it on a large round piece of cardboard (the cardboard from a frozen pizza would be an excellent choice). Tear a large sheet of Reynolds Wrap Aluminum Foil from the roll, place the cardboard on top of the sheet, and fold the foil upward, twisting the ends together at the very top. To make the gift tag, cut a long, narrow strip of white paper and write the gift recipient's name on it. Tie it at the top of the foil.

Snow paint

Add a few drops food coloring to water in a clean spray bottle and let the kids make holiday designs or greetings on the snow in your yard.

Wintry decorative touches

Make colored snowflakes by folding Melitta coffee filters into squares or triangles. Dip the corners of the filters into bowls of various colored water. Let the filters dry, then unfold.

Make ornaments or custom trays for serving holiday goodies. Cut decorative shapes out of cardboard, then cover the cardboard with Reynolds Wrap Aluminum Foil.

Christmas cleanup

Remove sticky Christmas tree sap from
your hands, or anywhere else it may
have stuck, with vegetable oil rubbed
into the area.

Store the greeting cards you received this Christmas in a GLAD Zipper Bag. Pull out the bag next

November to create your next greeting card list, then cut up the cards to make decorative gift tags.

Wrap it up

Reynolds Freezer Paper can be
custom decorated with stickers,
markers, or crayons and used as gift wrap.

Wrap an empty coffee can with decorated
Reynolds Freezer Paper, and fill the can with
candy, cookies, or baked goods. The can protects
the treats while shipping.

Cover the top of your dining
room or kitchen table in Reynolds
Freezer Paper and let the guests at
a child's birthday party write birthday wishes.
You can also invite guests to draw on the paper
while they wait for games and refreshments.

A long strip of Reynolds Freezer Paper can be just the place to write a birthday or congratulations greeting for a display banner. Just use markers, paints, or crayons on the dull side of the freezer paper, and hang.

PLAYTIME TRICKS
Organization ideas

Cut a hole in a clean, empty Clorox Bleach bottle and use it to store your children's crayons or small toys. If the edges are sharp, sand them down with a nail file.

Store cards, game pieces, and small toys in empty Pampers baby wipes containers.

To track whose toy is whose, mark the bottom of the toy with the child's name or initials using red Revlon Nail Enamel.

Stuffy stuffed animals

Give your child's dingy and smelly stuffed animals or cloth dolls a dry shampoo by rubbing the toys with a handful of cornstarch. Let the cornstarch sit 15 minutes, then brush or vacuum thoroughly.

Really smelly stuffed animals can be deodorized by placing them in a paper bag, adding baking soda, and shaking vigorously. Store overnight. If necessary, change the baking soda and repeat until odor is gone.

It's in the cards

Unstick sticky playing cards by dropping them into a brown paper bag and adding Johnson's Baby Powder. Shake the bag vigorously.

Pull a string

Run the string of a pull-toy through a GLAD flexible straw, and knot it at the end. This will prevent tangling.

 ### Tiny bubbles

Use a GLAD flexible straw as a bubble-blower. Cut one end on a diagonal and dip that end into the bubble liquid. Have the child blow out the other end.

Shout it out

Cut the bottom off a clean, empty Clorox Bleach bottle, remove the cap, and encourage the child to shout through the spout for a fun megaphone.

CUSTOM-COLOR FINGER PAINTS

Add ¼ cup cornstarch to 2 cups cold water and boil until the mixture thickens. Let cool slightly, then pour the mixture into small dishes or containers to make various paint colors. Add a few drops food coloring to each container. Also add a few drops Dawn Dishwashing Detergent to each bowl to help with cleanup. Make sure the paints are completely cool before using.

Walking tall

Punch 2 holes in the bottoms of 2 empty coffee cans and string a length of rope through them. Have the child stand on the cans and grab the ropes, holding tight.

A young Picasso

Make a disposable palette for paints by wrapping a piece of cardboard in Reynolds Wrap Aluminum Foil.

If you'd like to keep your child's artwork, spray it with a thin layer of Finesse Hair Spray.

Use Reach Dental Floss to hang children's artwork. Apply Elmer's glue to attach the floss to the back of the paper or punch a small hole in the artwork and thread the floss through.

SPORTS ALL AROUND
Just glovely
Help soften up the stiff leather of a new baseball mitt by adding Vaseline Petroleum Jelly to the palm. Rub in thoroughly and shape the glove around a ball. Secure with rubber bands overnight.

Lubricate and soften old, dried leather on a baseball glove by rubbing vegetable oil throughout.

Game time!
Nail an empty coffee can, with its bottom removed, above your garage door for a mini basketball hoop. Have the child toss Penn tennis balls instead of basketballs.

Wickets, anyone?
Help make your croquet wickets more visible in the lawn by running them through colorful GLAD flexible straws.

OTHER TRICKS AND TIPS
Bath time fun

Make a low-cost bath toy for very young children. Cut fun shapes in O-Cel-O Sponges and use these for kid cleanup time.

Add a little food coloring to a child's bathwater and he or she might start begging to take *more* baths.

Outfit coordination

A child just learning to dress on his or her own can be given a head start in matching things if you pack a large GLAD Zipper Bag with a complete outfit. The child can pick a bag for the day, then do it all alone.

A GLAD Zipper Bag makes an excellent organizer inside a baby bag to carry cotton balls, pacifiers, medicines, and the like. Store each group of items in a sandwich-size bag, then place the smaller bags in a large bag.

Suitcase smarts

Pack a child's suitcase using a large GLAD Zipper Bag for each day of the trip. Use 1 bag for a complete outfit, including socks and under- wear. This makes dressing a snap and helps keep suitcases tidy.

Caught in a jam

Carry a large GLAD Zipper Bag in your purse or bag to use as an emergency diaper-changing mat.

Chapter 7

In the Workshop

The ideal workshop would have one of every tool and special supplies tailor-made for each home project or repair task you might undertake. Unfortunately, most of us don't have that much room in our workshops (or money in our budgets). But by keeping just a few brand-name products on hand, you'll be amazed at all the fix-up, cleanup, and loosen-up chores you can handle all around the house!

TOOL TIME
Contain yourself

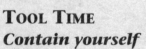
To organize small brads, screws, and other fasteners, nail the tops of baby food jars to the underside of a shelf in your workshop. Fill the jars, and screw them into the lids.

GLAD Zipper Bags are great for storing lighter items at your work-bench or in your toolbox, such as plastic fasteners and hose washers.

Chisels are expensive, and sharpening them can be a pain. Help them stay sharp by cutting a slit in a Penn tennis ball and storing the sharp end of the chisel in the slit.

Lost the cap to a tube of caulk? Keep it from drying out by closing it up in a GLAD Zipper Bag.

Hammer Softly

To prevent your hammer from denting soft woods, insert the face of the hammer into a slit cut into a Penn tennis ball before pounding nails.

If your workshop is in the basement or cellar, store your matches in a GLAD Zipper Bag to keep them dry.

The tightening of the screws

To fix screw holes that become too large to hold the screw, make a plug out of a cotton ball by soaking it in Elmer's glue and stuffing it into the hole. Let dry, then reinsert the screw.

Another way to help a loose screw is to break the top off a wooden Diamond safety match, insert the body of the match into the hole, then replace the screw.

You can also repair an enlarged screw hole by making a paste of sawdust and Elmer's glue. Fill the hole, let the glue dry overnight, then reinsert the screw.

 Tighten the screws in your eyeglasses with clear Revlon Nail Enamel. Just dab it on the screws and retighten. This will prevent future loosening.

LOOSEN UP
To loosen bolts or screws that have rusted, pour cola over them and wait a few minutes before trying again.

Loosen bolts by soaking cotton with club soda and wrapping it around the bolt with elastic. Wait a few minutes, then try again.

RUST BUSTERS
To remove rust from nuts and bolts, soak them overnight in cola. Rinse and scrub with steel wool or a Reach toothbrush.

Cola can also be used to scrub rust stains off of metals of all kinds. Saturate a steel wool pad with cola and apply to the rust with elbow grease.

Vaseline Petroleum Jelly is a great rust preventative for tools.

KEEP YOUR SCREWS LOOSE

If you're screwing into hard wood, rub the screws with Blistex Lip Balm first—the screws will go in much easier. This trick works with nails, too. If you don't have lip balm, try rubbing the nail or screw with Ivory bar soap. You can even dip nails or screws into Ivory liquid soap. You'll find that wood is less likely to split if the nails or screws are lubricated.

Just smear it on and wipe off the excess. This works on outdoor equipment as well.

 Another rust-dissolving wonder is white vinegar. Place rusty metal in a container of straight vinegar for several hours. Then scrub and rinse with plain water.

After you've cleaned your tools, prevent new rust from building up again by applying a thin film of Alberto VO5 Conditioning Hairdressing.

To prevent rust and keep filings from clogging a metal file, rub the file with a piece of Crayola Chalk.

Prevent new nuts, bolts, and screws from rusting by covering them with Alberto VO5 Conditioning Hairdressing before connecting them.

Apply clear Revlon Nail Enamel to toilet seat screws to protect against rust and lime deposits.

To prevent steel wool from rusting, store it in a GLAD Zipper Bag. Before storing, make sure the wool is totally dry.

OUT, DAMP SPOT!

Moisture, the culprit behind rust, can be prevented in one of the following ways:

- Keep a couple of pieces of Crayola Chalk in your toolbox.
- Place mothballs wherever moisture might attack your tools.
- Put a Downy Sheet at the bottom of your toolbox.

REMARKABLE REPAIRS
Perfect patches

To fill holes in wood, mix some instant coffee crystals with spackle or drywall compound, adding more until the color matches the wood. Smooth with a damp O-Cel-O sponge.

TAKE A SHINE TO YOUR TAPE MEASURE

Perform a little preventive maintenance on your metal tape measure by stretching it out, applying a thin layer of Simoniz Original Paste Wax, and buffing it to a shine. Your tape will uncoil and recoil more easily, and the wax will help prevent rust.

Another way to fill a small hole in wood is with a Diamond safety match. Cut off the tip, then pound the wooden match body into the hole. Cut or sand off the excess.

Small dents in hard wood can be filled with clear Revlon Nail Enamel, which lets the original color of the wood show through. Apply a coat, let dry, then apply more until the dent is leveled out.

After applying a patch to a window screen, dab the edges of the patch with clear Revlon Nail Enamel to strengthen it.

To fill small holes in drywall or plaster walls, use Pepsodent toothpaste. Allow the toothpaste to dry before painting.

For larger, dime-size holes in plaster walls, break off a piece of Crayola Chalk and insert into the hole. Then use patching plaster to cover.

For small cracks in plaster, make your own patching compound with Elmer's glue and baking soda. Mix enough glue with the baking soda to make a paste, then fill cracks and let dry before painting.

Fix holes in linoleum by choosing a Crayola Crayon that matches the linoleum. Melt the crayon in a microwave and pour into the hole. Let cool, and wax or polish as usual.

Get rid of scratches

Fine scratches in eyeglasses can sometimes be removed by using a paste made of Johnson's Baby Powder and water to polish the lenses.

To repair scratches in furniture, choose a Crayola Crayon that matches the wood. Slightly warm the crayon with a hair dryer, rub it into the scratch, and buff the area with a soft cloth.

You can fill cracks and small gaps in wood, metal, and plastic by sprinkling baking soda into the crack and then dripping Krazy Glue over it until the gap is filled.

Revival time

 Dry wood, such as paneling, can be revived by applying a treatment of Alberto VO5 Conditioning Hairdressing. Rub on with a soft cloth, and buff dry.

A broken spring in a battery-operated device can ruin it—unless you fold a small piece of Reynolds Wrap Aluminum Foil and use it to fill the gap.

If the silver backing of a mirror wears off, tape a piece of Reynolds Wrap Aluminum Foil to the back with the shiny side toward the mirror.

If the glue on a floor tile has dried out and the tile is coming up, you may be able to revive it. Cover the tile with a sheet of Reynolds Wrap Aluminum Foil and heat with an iron until the glue is melted. Place a heavy object on the tile until the glue dries again.

Squelching squeaks

 Silence a squeaky floorboard by dribbling Elmer's glue into the crack. Let dry overnight before walking on the floor again.

Another solution for squeaky floors is to sprinkle Johnson's Baby Powder into the crack, sweeping it in with a broom. The powder acts as a lubricant between the boards.

To fix a screeching water faucet, coat the threads of the faucet stem with Vaseline Petroleum Jelly. (Just be sure to turn off the water supply to the sink first!)

 Alberto VO5 Conditioning Hairdressing can also be used to lubricate a screeching water faucet. Use a Q-Tip Cotton Swab to rub on the faucet threads, then reassemble.

SILENCE!

Do squeaky doors have you coming unhinged? Try one of the following:
•Spray the hinge with Pam cooking spray.
  •Dab some Alberto VO5 Conditioning Hairdressing on the culprit.
  •Spray Pledge furniture polish on the hinge.
  •Work some Vaseline Petroleum Jelly into the noisy hinge.

UNSTICKING STICKY SITUATIONS
Kitchen binds
To make your refrigerator racks slide smoothly, apply a little Alberto VO5 Conditioning Hairdressing to the edges.

Another way to make refrigerator racks slide easily is to rub Vaseline Petroleum Jelly on their sides.

Bathroom bungles
Use a little Alberto VO5 Conditioning Hairdressing to make pipe fittings go together smoothly.

If your plumber's helper slips while plunging the toilet, smear some Vaseline Petroleum Jelly around the ring for a better seal.

If the sliding doors to your medicine cabinet are stiff and noisy, lubricate the tracks with a bit of Alberto VO5 Conditioning Hairdressing.

Make your shower curtains glide more smoothly by rubbing Vaseline Petroleum Jelly on the shower rod.

Wood works

Rub Ivory bar soap in the tracks of a
wooden window to keep it from
sticking. Alberto VO5 Conditioning
Hairdressing will also help to unstick a sticky
window.

 Sticky drawers will come unstuck if
you rub some Alberto VO5 Conditioning Hairdressing in their tracks.

Another way to lubricate drawer
slides is with a tube of Blistex Lip
Balm. The tube fits perfectly in the
drawer tracks.

To make sawing wood easier, spray your handsaw
with WD-40 before you begin cutting.

LOCK, STOCK, AND MATCHSTICK

Here's a cure for a frozen door lock: Wearing work gloves
or oven mitts, heat the key with a Dia-
mond match, then insert it into the lock.
Repeat this until the heat from the key
transfers to the lock so you can open it.
    For a sticky key, just spray it with a bit
of Pam cooking spray.

Vaseline Petroleum Jelly will also help prevent a saw from becoming bound by a piece of tough wood. Smear it on both sides of the blade before sawing.

PLUS SIDE TO PAINTING
Colorful cleanup

An easy way to protect doorknobs and other fixtures from paint drips is to wrap Reynolds Wrap Aluminum Foil around them. The foil adapts to a variety of shapes and comes off easily when you're done painting.

If you're a really messy painter, try slicking down your hair with Alberto VO5 Conditioning Hairdressing before you start painting. Paint sprays and drips will wash out in a jiffy.

When painting with a roller, save cleanup time by lining your paint tray with Reynolds Wrap Aluminum Foil before adding the paint. When you're through, simply throw the foil away.

Make your personal cleanup easier by rubbing exposed areas of your skin with Vaseline Petroleum Jelly before you start painting. Drips should wash off more easily.

Here's a tip for disposing of unused paint: Mix some Fresh Step cat litter with the paint and leave the top off until it dries, then dispose.

Brush magic

After cleaning your paintbrushes, help keep them soft by rinsing them in water with a capful of Final Touch fabric softener added. Hang to dry.

Before you throw out those old, hardened paintbrushes, try soaking them in hot lemon juice or white vinegar. As the bristles soften, comb through them with a wire brush or fork.

To keep the ends of your paintbrushes in shape, cut slits in the plastic lid of a coffee can, and stick the brush handles up through the bottom. Fill the can with paint thinner, and replace the lid.

If you're not done with a painting job, wrap your paintbrushes with Reynolds Wrap Aluminum Foil and put them in the refrigerator or freezer until you're ready to go back to work.

When performing a touch-up job on a very small area of your furniture or walls, use a Q-Tip Cotton Swab as your paintbrush. Just throw the Q-Tip away when you're finished.

SAFETY FIRST

To prevent cuts from loose razor blades in your toolbox, stick a blade inside an empty book of Diamond matches, with the sharp edge tucked in where the matches normally attach.

To make cleanup easier when installing fiberglass insulation, rub your hands and arms with Johnson's Baby Powder first. When finished, use a hose to rinse off any lingering particles.

CHALK IT UP

Just as chalk keeps a pool cue from slipping, rubbing a piece of Crayola Chalk on your screwdriver tip will keep it from sliding off the screw.

Baking soda makes an excellent fire extinguisher for small fires in the shop—or anywhere else, for that matter. Keep a box handy and sprinkle on the base of a fire to put it out.

Chapter 8

Garage Magic

If a man's home is his castle, the car must be his trusty steed and the garage his stable. Unfortunately, most garages end up *looking* like a stable, and the trusty steed is more like the old gray mare. To fix that, here are some quick and easy solutions to keeping

the buggy and the barn in tip-top shape using everyday products you probably already have around the house.

Cleaning Up's Not Hard to Do
Interior ideas

Get winter's salt stains out of your car carpeting with a mixture of equal parts vinegar and water. Just scrub in the solution, and rinse thoroughly.

To remove oil and grease on vinyl seats, sprinkle baking soda on a damp sponge and scrub. Rinse, then wipe clean.

Other spots on upholstery can be cleaned with a paste of baking soda and water. Rub the paste into the stain, let dry, and vacuum.

 Revive old, worn rubber floor mats by shining them with Griffin Liquid Wax Shoe Polish after cleaning them.

Use baking soda to safely clean your car's vinyl seats, floor mats, lights, chrome, windows, and tires. Sprinkle onto a damp sponge, scrub, and rinse.

Revive dry leather with an application of Johnson's Baby Oil. Wipe on a small amount with a clean cloth, rub in, and let dry. Then buff to shine, removing any excess oil.

HOMEMADE CAR UPHOLSTERY CLEANER

Make a stiff foam by mixing ¼ cup Ivory liquid soap in 1 cup warm water and beating the mixture with an eggbeater. Spread the foam over the upholstery with a sponge, using circular, overlapping strokes. Let it dry, then vacuum the soil away.

You can clean your car dashboard
with a Pampers baby wipe.

What a body!

Faux wood paneling on cars can be polished with
brown Griffin Wax Shoe Paste to restore its original factory luster.

Buff your car's polish with a bit of
cornstarch on a clean cloth.

Remove dead bugs from your car by pouring full-
strength vinegar on a cloth and scrubbing.

Another cleaning solution for bugs is
cola, poured directly on the splattered
bugs or applied with a car scrub brush.

Sticky tar can be removed from your car's
bumpers, chrome, and body by covering it with
vegetable oil, letting it soak in, then washing off.

Another way to remove tar spots is to
cover them with mayonnaise. Wait
several minutes, then scrub away.

Spray WD-40 on tar spots to loosen them before
washing.

A Crayola Crayon can cover scratches on your car's finish. Match the color of the crayon to your car, and rub it over the scratches. Buff the area with a cloth.

DREAM SCHEMES FOR CHROME

Shine the chrome on any car using full-strength vinegar on a soft polishing cloth. The vinegar leaves no spots behind.

Another good chrome polish is a bit of Alberto VO5 Conditioning Hairdressing on a clean cloth. Rub on and buff.

To shine your hubcaps, drop a Polident Denture Cleanser tablet into water, and scrub hubcaps with the solution. Rinse with clean water.

MAKE TIRES SPARKLE

Trisodium phosphate will remove any stain from a whitewall tire, but if phosphates are banned in your area or you prefer not to use them, substitute baking soda. Apply the baking soda with a damp cloth, and use a scrub brush to work it into discolored areas of the whitewall. Rinse with clean water.

Best bets for bumpers

To get rid of rust spots on bumpers, scrub with cola, using a wadded-up piece of Reynolds Wrap Aluminum Foil as a scrubber.

Been playing "bumper cars" with other vehicles? Remove scuffs on bumpers with baking soda and a damp O-Cel-O sponge.

Once the bumpers and grille are clean, spray Pam cooking spray on them to make it easier to clean off rust and bugs the next time.

A STICKY SITUATION

Changed your mind about that old bumper sticker? Use Cutex nail polish remover to soften the sticker, then carefully scrape it off.

You can also take off old bumper stickers by covering them with vegetable oil. Allow the oil to sit for 15 to 30 minutes, then scrape off the sticker.

Another great way to remove an old bumper sticker is to heat it with a hair dryer to loosen the glue, then peel it off. Works like magic!

HOMEMADE WINDOW WASHER FLUID

Here's a recipe for making your own windshield washer fluid:

Recipe Box

1 cup rubbing alcohol
2 tablespoons Ivory liquid soap
1 gallon water
1 or 2 drops blue food coloring

Mix well, and store in a clearly marked plastic container.

VINEGAR

Remove the price sticker sheet from a new car by soaking it with vinegar from a spray bottle. Wait a few minutes, then peel off. The vinegar can help rub off any remaining glue residue as well.

Clear view

If your car windows develop a film on the inside, clean them with ½ cup ammonia in a gallon of water. The ammonia cuts grease, but it's noxious, so leave the doors open while doing this.

To clean grease and grime from your windshield, pour club soda on a clean cloth, and polish.

Club Soda

Another good windshield cleaner is ¼ cup vinegar in a bucket of warm water.

When windshield wipers leave marks on your clean windshield, wipe them down with a Pampers baby wipe.

CLEAR THE AIR

Freshen up your car's smell with a Downy Sheet tucked under the seat, in the glove compartment, or in the visor.

Perform an overnight deodorizing treatment on your automobile by soaking a piece of bread in vinegar and leaving it in the car, with the windows closed, overnight.

Here's another way to remove car odors: Simply sprinkle baking soda on the seats and carpets and let it sit at least ½ hour. Vacuum.

COLD WEATHER CAR CURES

Car locks frozen on a cold winter morning? Try blowing a hot hair dryer on them until they loosen up.

To help keep car locks from freezing, oil them with a couple drops of Mobil 1 synthetic motor oil (not regular oil). Work the key in and out a few times to spread the oil around.

If your car doors tend to freeze shut in the winter, coat the gaskets around the doors with vegetable oil.

Avoid frosted car windows on a cold morning by rubbing them in the evening with a sponge dipped in a solution of 2 tablespoons salt in 2 cups water.

Fill a small cloth bag or scrap of cloth with salt and hold it securely closed. Dampen the bag with water, then rub it on the outside of the windshield to keep snow and ice from adhering.

Another windshield treatment is a spray of 3 parts vinegar to 1 part water. Mix these together in a spray bottle and use on windows in the evening to keep frost from developing overnight.

 Keep a bag of Fresh Step cat litter in your car trunk to provide traction in case you get stuck on the ice.

If you don't have a garage and a snowstorm is coming, cover your car's side mirrors with a GLAD Zipper Bag held in place by clothespins or elastic bands. You won't have to scrape them later.

BEST BETS FOR BATTERIES

A paste made of 3 parts baking soda to 1 part water is useful for removing corrosion buildup from your car's battery terminals.

You can also clean battery terminals with cola. Pour the soda directly on, or dip a piece of Reynolds Wrap Aluminum Foil in the cola and scrub.

Once battery terminals are clean, put a coating of Vaseline Petroleum Jelly on to keep corrosion from building up in the future.

 You can also use Blistex Lip Balm to protect battery terminals.

THE BIG SPILL

Salt works as an absorbent to soak up a garage spill. Pour it over the spill and allow it to soak up the liquid, then remove.

To clean up oil, brake fluid, transmission fluid, and other spills on your garage floor, cover the spill with clean Fresh Step cat litter. Allow it to absorb the liquid for at least 1 hour, then clean up.

Another dry cleanup treatment for garage spills is to sprinkle on a mixture of baking soda and corn meal. Allow the spill to soak in, then sweep or vacuum up.

If spills leave a stain on your concrete floor, sprinkle baking soda on it, let stand, and scrub with a wet brush.

For tougher stains on garage floors, use Electrasol Automatic Dishwashing Detergent or Tide Powder detergent. Cover the spill with enough to soak up the liquid, let sit for a while, then wash with hot water and a stiff brush, wearing rubber gloves.

Another solution for tough stains is to pour paint thinner over them. Then pour on Fresh Step cat litter, allow it to absorb the thinner, and sweep up.

Neutralize acid from leaking batteries by applying baking soda to the spill. One pound of soda will neutralize 1 pint of acid.

Winter Wonders

Snow won't stick to your shovel if you coat it with Simoniz Original Paste Wax.

 You can also coat your snow shovel with vegetable oil to give it a snow-resistant surface.

Spread rock salt easily with a dispenser made from a clean Clorox Bleach bottle. Cut a hole opposite the handle, below the spout, to pour in the rock salt. Then shake to dispense as needed.

Loosen up stiff, rusted buckles on boots, snow gear, and other outdoor clothes and equipment by spraying them with WD-40.

 Sprinkle clean Fresh Step cat litter on icy sidewalks and driveways to provide traction.

KEEP YOURSELF CLEAN

Keep a supply of Pampers baby
wipes in the car to clean gas off
your hands after pumping.

Use a little Dawn Dishwashing
Detergent on your hands to cut
grease and grime when working on
the car.

Tuck a few Pampers baby wipes in
a GLAD Zipper Bag to take along
on trips for cleaning messy fingers
and faces.

MUST BE GONE

A damp, musty garage can be helped with this
simple remedy: Add ½ inch baking soda to the
bottom of a grocery bag with handles, and hang
from the rafters. Change every 3 months.

You can refresh musty old magazines
found in cellars or garages if the
pages aren't stuck together. Lay the
magazines out in the sun for a day.
Then sprinkle baking soda on pages, and let sit
for an hour or so. Brush off.

RV TIPS FOR GREAT TRIPS

 Deodorize and help remove mineral deposits in an RV water tank by flushing periodically with 1 cup baking soda in 1 gallon warm water. Drain and flush the tank before refilling.

To dissolve solids and control odor in toilets of RVs or boats, pour a small box of baking soda into the tank after each cleaning.

MAKE YOUR OWN

You can improvise emergency lights by wrapping reflective tape around empty coffee cans.

 When you need a funnel in a hurry, make one from a clean, empty Clorox Bleach bottle. Cut the bottle in half, discard the bottom, and remove the cap from the top.

Need a pan to catch oil drips while working on the car? Flatten a cardboard box, cover it with Reynolds Wrap Aluminum Foil, and tape it down with duct tape.

Make a windshield sun reflector for your car by cutting a piece of cardboard to fit it, covering the cardboard with Reynolds Wrap Aluminum Foil, and taping down with duct tape.

OTHER TRICKS AND TIPS

If you keep bumping into your garage wall, hang a Penn tennis ball from the ceiling at the exact spot where your windshield should be when you stop. When you hit it, you're home free.

When you need to lubricate something that is way out of reach, stick a GLAD flexible straw over the end of the spout of a fine-nose oil can.

Keep your trailer hitch from getting scratched by cutting a slit in a Penn tennis ball and putting it over the ball of the hitch.

If your key won't turn in the ignition, try spraying a bit of WD-40 into the lock to lubricate it, then try again.

Chapter 9

The Garden Shed

Do you ever feel as if you spend more money on your lawn and garden than on yourself? By the time you purchase all the sprays, chemicals, and tools you're supposed to have, you may spend a small fortune. Instead, you could save a lot of that money by using some of the brand-name products you already have in your home. Here are some great tips for keeping your yard *and* your wallet looking healthy.

THE GRASS IS ALWAYS GREENER

To help new grass seed grow in your yard, first mix it with 2 tablespoons cold, strong tea, and store it in the refrigerator for 5 days. Spread the grass seed on newspapers to dry another 2 days, then apply to the lawn.

Get rid of those nettlesome weeds between the cracks of sidewalks and driveways: Boil 1 quart water and add 2 tablespoons salt and 5 table- spoons vinegar. While still hot, pour this mixture directly onto the weeds.

 Keep weeds and grass out of the spaces between path and patio bricks by pour- ing undiluted vinegar directly on them. When a weed pops up, spray it directly with vinegar.

ORGANIC LAWN FERTILIZER

1 cup Scope mouthwash
1 cup Epsom salts
1 cup ammonia
Enough beer to make 1 quart

Add this mixture to a garden sprayer, and spray your lawn twice early in the season.

A less elaborate version of the same lawn fertilizer is to mix 1 cup Epsom salts and 1 cup ammonia. Mix 2 table- spoons of this mixture with 2 gallons water. Use a watering can to apply the fertilizer to the lawn.

Grass won't stick to your lawn mower blades as much if you coat them with one of these: Vaseline Petroleum Jelly, vegetable oil, or Alberto VO5 Conditioning Hairdressing. These products will also help prevent rust on the blades.

QUICK TRICK BEFORE PLANTING

Test your soil acidity: Add a pinch of baking soda to 1 tablespoon soil. If it fizzes, the soil's pH level is probably less than 5.0.

When your coffee can is empty, punch numerous small holes in the plastic lid. Fill the can with fertilizer or grass seed, add the lid, and shake the can while walking around your lawn.

SEEDLINGS, SEEDS, AND CUTTINGS

Gather your nursery flat containers from last season and reuse for seedlings, but first protect against disease by washing them with Dawn Dishwashing Detergent. Rinse with undiluted vinegar.

Mix your carrot seeds with coffee grounds before sowing them. The coffee protects against root maggots and adds nutrients to the soil.

If you keep your seedlings on a windowsill before they head outside, surround them with a trifolded piece of cardboard covered with Reynolds Wrap Aluminum Foil to bring in as much light as possible.

Store leftover seeds in small GLAD Zipper Bags in a cool, dry place.

If seedlings begin to mold while starting them in a damp medium, clean them with a solution of 1 part vinegar to 9 parts water, and transfer them to a new container. Spritz the seeds regularly with this diluted spray while awaiting germination.

SOME SEEDLING SCIENCE

When you prepare seedlings, make a batch of clear gelatin in a small, clear glass baking pan. Drop seeds on the top before the gelatin hardens completely. Children can watch the roots grow down as the plants grow up.

Seedlings in the garden may need protection from cold night air. Place a Clorox Bleach bottle with the bottom cut out over the transplants. Take the bottle off during the day; replace it at night.

ORGANIC HERBICIDE

Here is a basic organic herbicide that works well on most plants prone to disease. Mix 1 gallon vinegar with 1 cup orange oil and ¼ cup Ivory liquid soap. Add mixture to a garden sprayer, and spray on plants.

To keep cuttings upright in a jar of water, stretch a piece of Reynolds Wrap Aluminum Foil over the jar and poke holes in the foil using a toothpick. Insert the cutting stems through the holes.

Plant your seeds in the egg pods of a cardboard egg carton. When the plants have grown enough to go outside, plant them, carton and all.

GARDEN GOODNESS
Vital vegetables

When melons get big enough, lift them off the ground and put them on top of an upside down coffee can. Press the can into the soil. The can will help repel insects, and your melons may ripen more quickly.

Sprinkle baking soda lightly around tomato plants to lower acidity and sweeten the tomatoes.

Protect new tomato plants by making a ring out of a coffee can. Press the ring into the soil around the plant.

Cut a hole opposite the handle of a clean Clorox Bleach bottle, and thread a belt through the handle. Put on the belt to use as a bucket for dropping in berries as you harvest.

Keep a late-season frost away from your new plants by insulating them with a milk jug. Cut off the bottom, and use the top. Sink the jug into the ground on nights when it might get cold.

Crushed eggshells make an excellent fertilizer for vegetable or flower gardens. Working the eggshells into the garden soil also helps to aerate the soil.

CABBAGE COSTUME

Wrap a cabbage head when it is new in the leg of a pair of No nonsense panty hose. The nylon will stretch to accommodate the cabbage and will keep worms out without blocking sunlight, air, or water—though the other vegetables in the garden may make fun of it!

Kill poison ivy

Mix 3 pounds salt with 1 gallon soapy water. Use a garden sprayer to apply this to poison ivy plants.

Plant recovery

Brighten fading green outdoor plants and bushes by mixing 1 teaspoon baking soda, 1 teaspoon Epsom salts, ½ teaspoon clear ammonia, and 1 gallon water. Apply 1 quart per average rosebush-size shrub.

TAKING CARE OF GARDEN TOOLS

Wherever you store your garden tools, keep a gallon of sand mixed with 1 quart Mobil 1 motor oil nearby. When putting the tools away, stab them into the sand to clean off dirt, and oil the tool at the same time. This prevents rusting, too.

Rose Rx

Stir 3 tablespoons vinegar into 1 gallon water and store in your garden sprayer. Use on roses daily to control fungal diseases such as black spot.

Soak some onions in water in your garden sprayer. Let sit overnight, and use this mixture to spray your roses if their color has faded. The mixture brightens color and perks up flowers.

Compost control

Control odors in your compost pile by sprinkling it every now and then with baking soda.

Clean garden containers

Clay flowerpots develop stains over time. Fill them with enough cold water to cover the stains, then add half as much vinegar. Let them soak overnight, then scrub with soap and water and rinse thoroughly.

If you have white stepping stones on your garden path, clean them occasionally by scrubbing with a solution of ¼ cup baking soda added to 1 gallon warm water.

FERTILIZING SPRAY

Keep this organic spray on hand as a foliage helper.

- 1 ounce molasses
- 1 cup manure-base compost tea
- 1 ounce liquid seaweed
- 1 ounce vinegar

Recipe Box

Add the above ingredients to a gallon of water. Put this liquid into a garden sprayer and use it on green plants in your garden.

Give the birdbath a bath

Clean a cement birdbath by sprinkling it with baking soda. Scrub, and rinse.

When the garden comes inside

 If you want to add a bit of color to white cut flowers, mix a few drops of food coloring in warm water and add the flowers. Overnight, they will turn color.

Lengthen flower stems too short for your vase by inserting the stems into a GLAD flexible straw and cutting to the appropriate length.

A simple preservative for a vase of cut flowers is 1 quart warm water to which you've added 2 tablespoons vinegar and 1 teaspoon sugar.

 Extend the life of freshly cut flowers by adding ¼ teaspoon Clorox Bleach to a quart of water or by adding ¼ cup baking soda to 1 quart water.

When displaying cut roses, place them in a mixture of 2 tablespoons vinegar added to 1 gallon water. Change the solution every 2 or 3 days.

Placing cut flowers in a vase with this mixture will help preserve them if you intend to dry them out: Mix 1 tablespoon sugar and 2 drops Clorox Bleach to 1 cup water. Let the liquid completely evaporate, and the shape and color will be preserved.

BUG-CONTROL BASICS

If your crop of cucumbers or squash seems threatened by munching bugs, cut up small strips of Reynolds Wrap Aluminum Foil and use them as mulch. The shiny substance scares away some light-sensitive pests.

Make your own organic insecticide: Mix 2 tablespoons Dawn Dishwashing Detergent in 1 gallon water and add to a spray bottle. Spray tops and bottoms of leaves in the mornings or evenings.

SAP THOSE SUCKERS

Here's an insecticide spray that targets chewing or sucking pests: Combine 3 garlic bulbs, 1 small onion, 1 tablespoon cayenne pepper, ½ teaspoon Dawn Dishwashing Detergent, and 1 quart water. Blend on low speed, then strain through a Melitta coffee filter. Add to a spray bottle, and spray plants thoroughly when you see evidence of chewing.

Awful aphids

Protect your precious plants from aphids by spraying the plants with this anti-aphid mixture: Combine 1 cup Rite Aid rubbing alcohol and 1 cup water. Put liquid in a mister, and lightly spray plants. (Do not use this mixture on fruits or vegetables or on plants that have very delicate leaves.)

Give cabbage worms a dusting

Mix together 1 cup flour and ½ cup salt. Dust this mixture on cabbage, broccoli, and cauliflower leaves to protect them from worms. It's best to apply the powder when plants are dewy or damp.

Control cutworms

Keep cutworms away from your favorite plants by making a barrier out of a Clorox Bleach bottle. First cut off the bottom and top of the jug. Then cut the bottle into rings, each 3 inches wide. Sink each plastic ring into the soil about 2 inches, leaving 1 inch above the soil.

Ant traps and tricks

Control ants around your garden by locating their hill and sprinkling it liberally with Johnson's Baby Powder. The ants will try to relocate their hill, but keep sprinkling and eventually they'll get the message and move on to your neighbor's yard!

Keep ants from coming into your home by circling the foundation of your house with a mixture of 2 parts 20 Mule Team Borax to 1 part sugar.

Slimy slugs

Fill a spray bottle with equal parts vinegar and water. Go into your garden at night to find the slugs and squirt them directly.

MAKE ANTS WALK THE LINE

There's a basic theory out there that ants either don't like to or can't cross over certain lines. Either they are repelled by the substance or they can't follow each other when the lead ant steps into something unexpected. Wherever you see ants coming into your home, block their entry with a line of dried out coffee grounds, Crayola Chalk, vinegar, or a bit of all-purpose flour. Step back and watch which ones toe the line—or don't!

You can also kill a slug by dumping some salt directly on the slimy critter. Watch the slug for a few minutes, then dump some more salt on it just to be sure.

Make a slug trap by setting out a pie pan or another shallow dish of beer or cola in the garden. Slugs will come to visit in the night and likely drown in their drink.

When bugs bug people

 When working outdoors during mosquito time, tie a Downy Sheet around one of your belt loops. The scent from the fabric softener sheet will keep mosquitoes away.

Are you tired of being forced inside because mosquitoes are bugging you during a nice outdoor meal? Try dabbing some vinegar at the pulse points on your body to keep mosquitoes away.

At a picnic, rub Johnson's Baby Oil on your face and any exposed parts of your arms and legs to keep gnats away.

Bee gone!

If you'd rather not use insecticide spray inside your home, aim a bottle of Finesse Hair Spray at wasps, hornets, yellow jackets, or bees who have made an unexpected visit.

Cocky cockroaches

Create a mixture of half cornstarch and half plaster of paris. Sprinkle this around cracks and crevices in your home to control cockroaches, which will eat it and turn into little bug statues as a result.

Another cockroach solution: Briefly heat 1 teaspoon boric acid with 1 teaspoon corn syrup in a microwave. Stir to make sure boric acid dissolves. Place this mixture in bottle caps around your home, or use an eyedropper to apply it to cracks. Keep pets and children away.

GARDEN PATROL FOR ANIMAL CONTROL

Keep the cat out

Cats can wreak havoc on your garden by using it as a litter box. Soak wads of newspaper with white vinegar. Scatter them where cats have been to discourage repeat visits.

Oh, deer

Cut Ivory bar soap in half and put each half in a piece of No nonsense panty hose. Tie the bundle to a  stake about 4 feet above the ground. Place the stakes throughout your garden.

If deer are nibbling at the bark of a young tree, protect it by wrapping the trunk with Reynolds Wrap Aluminum Foil. The foil should be at least as high as your waist.

Holy moley

 In the fall when you plant bulbs, be sure to dust them first with medicated Johnson's Baby Powder. Munching critters such as moles and squirrels will be kept at bay.

HELP FOR HOUSEHOLD PLANTS

Water your houseplants with club soda that has gone flat. It serves as a fertilizer.

If your houseplants look like an insect is nibbling them, mix ½ cup Dawn Dishwashing Detergent in water and spray both sides of the plant's leaves.

HOMEMADE PLANT FOOD

1 teaspoon baking powder
½ teaspoon ammonia
1 tablespoon Epsom salts
1 teaspoon salt
1 gallon water

Recipe Box

Mix ingredients together and store in a spray bottle. Shake well before using. Spray household plants once a month.

Mix cooled brewed tea with the same amount of water and use this to water household ferns.

Feed 2 tablespoons vegetable oil at the root of your household palm or fern once a month to give it a boost.

To clean dusty houseplant leaves, add ¼ cup dry milk to 2 cups water. Dampen a soft cloth, and wipe on.

DRY MILK POWDER

Mayonnaise

Apply a small dab of Vaseline Petroleum Jelly to plant leaves to clean them. You can even use mayonnaise for this task.

Help household plants that need a lot of sunlight: Line a windowsill with Reynolds Wrap Aluminum Foil to increase the sun's reflection. This is great for cacti and geraniums.

Mix ¼ cup vinegar with 1 gallon compost tea and spray household plants regularly to invigorate them.

Line a pot that has lots of drainage holes with a Melitta coffee filter to prevent soil from leaking through while allowing water to seep out.

Mix ¼ cup baking soda in 1 quart water and use to scrub out your indoor flowerpots.

When transplanting plants into clay pots, brush the pots with a thin layer of baking soda before adding the soil. This helps the dirt stay fresh longer.

Mix coffee grounds into your potting soil for household plants, or add them to topsoil in the garden as a fertilizer.

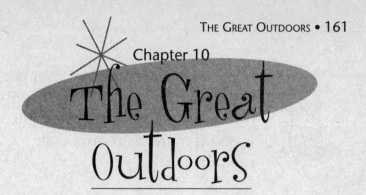

Chapter 10
The Great Outdoors

When vacation time rolls around, there's always a lot of work to do, whether you're heading out on the road or just preparing to hang out in the backyard. But you probably have better uses for your money than buying a lot of specialty products to take care of your recreational gear. Fortunately, most tasks can be taken care of with products you already own. Here are some great ways to get your gear ready for those relaxing days on the water, the links, and around the campfire.

'ROUND THE CAMPFIRE
Cooking out
Propane lantern mantles can be made to last longer if they are first soaked in undiluted vinegar for several hours. Allow to dry, then light.

If you coat the bottoms of your pots with Dawn Dishwashing Detergent before you start cooking, soot will wash off more easily after your campfire meals.

To clean dirty pots and pans while on a camping trip, scrunch up Reynolds Wrap Aluminum Foil into a ball and use as a pot scrubber.

Pitch a tent
Pounding in tent stakes can be made easier by spraying the stakes with WD-40 before hammering them into the ground.

Deodorize canvas bags or any bags that have developed a musty smell by sprinkling the insides with salt, zipping them up, and leaving them overnight. Remove the salt in the morning, and allow the bag to air out.

To kill mold and mildew on a tent, scrub all surfaces with a mixture of 1 cup Clorox Bleach in 1 gallon water. Wear rubber gloves to protect your hands.

A mildewed tent can also be cleaned by wiping the mildewed areas with vinegar and then letting the tent dry out in the sun.

Clean and eliminate static on plastic tarps and other plastic outdoor equipment coverings by adding 1 tablespoon undiluted vinegar to 1 gallon water. This may also reduce the amount of dust attracted to the plastic covering.

Knots in tent ropes and other camping gear will untangle more easily if you sprinkle them with cornstarch.

Zippers on outdoor equipment are prone to sticking because of rust. Spray them with WD-40 and work the zipper up and down to drive out moisture, remove rust, and lubricate.

On the trail

Water kept in a closed container can taste stale. Keep your hiking supply of water fresh by adding a few drops of vinegar to the bottle or canteen. The vinegar will also make the water a better thirst quencher.

Before heading out for a hike, prevent blisters on any areas of your feet that are prone to them by lubricating with Vaseline Petroleum Jelly.

Super storage ideas

Keep your toilet paper dry when you're camping by storing it in a clean, empty coffee can with a plastic top on it.

 Store miscellaneous camping items (food, medicine, batteries, and so on) in individual GLAD Zipper Bags to keep them dry and organized.

BEST BETS FOR BOATS

Remove tree sap and bugs from your boat's windshield with WD-40.

CAN-DO FIRE STARTER

An empty coffee can makes a great fire starter. Cut off both ends of the can, and punch holes around the bottom. Stand the can in your campfire or grill, fill with charcoal, and soak with lighter fluid. When the coals are lit and burning well, remove the can with oven mitts, leaving the hot coals behind.

Use Vaseline Petroleum Jelly to lubricate boat fittings and to prevent rust from developing.

Brighten unlacquered brass on boats with a paste of baking soda and lemon juice. Rub on, and let dry. Rinse well with warm water.

Clean stains on fiberglass boat bodies by scrubbing with baking soda on a damp O-Cel-O sponge. For tough stains, leave wet baking soda on and wipe away when it dries.

Clean, empty Clorox Bleach bottles make great buoys for boating or swimming areas. Tighten the cap, tie a rope around the handle, and attach the other end of the rope to a second bottle filled with sand.

THE LAST STRAW FOR CAMP COOKING

Store condiments for camp cooking (salt, pepper, spices, and so on) in GLAD flexible straws. Fold over the end of the straw and secure it closed with a small rubber band. Pour the spice into the straw, then fold over and secure the other end with another rubber band. Label the straws with a marking pen.

Remove corrosion from stainless-steel fixtures on boats with Electrasol Automatic Dishwashing Detergent and a scrub brush dipped in water.

WD-40 is a great all-purpose cleaner for fittings, vinyl, mats, brass, and many other boat parts. It even removes tar and barnacles from the hull.

KEEP BIKES ROLLING

Remove old decals from a bicycle frame by spraying them with WD-40. Let the solution sit for a few minutes, then peel or scrape off the decal.

Clean the rust from bike handlebars or tire rims by making a paste of 6 tablespoons salt and 2 tablespoons lemon juice. Apply the paste to the rusted areas with a dry cloth, then rub, rinse, and dry thoroughly.

To clean bike chains, chrome, and other fixtures, spray them with WD-40 and wipe off with a rag. This also lubricates and prevents rust.

Bikers can keep dust and dirt from sticking to their goggles by spraying the lenses with Static Guard before hitting the road.

A quick spray of WD-40 may be all you need to stop squeaks on bicycles, roller blades, swing sets, exercise machines, and any other outdoor equipment with moving parts.

A FINE KETTLE OF FISHING TIPS

Keep fishhooks from rusting between fishing trips by sticking them in a cork and submerging the cork in baking soda.

 Make your own imitation fish egg bait by cutting an O-Cel-O sponge into small pieces and smearing the sponge bits with Vaseline Petroleum Jelly.

Add baking soda to hollow fishing lures to give them spin in the water.

 Rub a freshly caught fish with vinegar before cleaning and scaling it. The scaling will go easier, and the vinegar will help control the fishy odor on your hands.

Keep a large box of baking soda in your boat as a precaution in case of small oil, gas, or engine fires. Sprinkle soda onto the flames from a safe distance.

Don't throw out those old coffee grounds when leaving on a fishing trip—put them back in the empty coffee can and carry your live worms there.

PATIO AND PICNIC

Wash mildewed areas of wicker furniture with a solution of warm water and salt, then rinse and dry well.

Clean lawn furniture at the start of the season with ¼ cup baking soda in 1 quart warm water. Wipe, and rinse.

Control the flames when fat drips on your grill coals by keeping a spray bottle of 1 teaspoon baking soda mixed with 1 pint water handy. Lightly spray onto coals when flames shoot up.

To make cleanup of your barbecue grill easier, apply vegetable oil before you start cooking, while the grill is still cool.

To clean indoor or outdoor grills, pour cold coffee over the grill when it's cool. Wipe clean.

Soak a mildewed or smelly plastic tablecloth in a solution of baking soda and water, then set out in the sun to dry.

 Picnic jugs and coolers often take on musty or mildewy smells. Rinse smelly items with undiluted vinegar, then wash with soap and water to clean thoroughly. Rinse.

GLORIFY YOUR GOLF GEAR

Spiff up your golf balls with a bath in 1 cup water and ¼ cup ammonia.

To clean golf balls, clubs, and carts, spray on WD-40 and wipe with a clean cloth.

OUTDOOR FURNITURE

If you've discovered your outdoor wicker furniture has mildewed while being stored over the winter, get rid of the mildew by washing the area with a mixture of vinegar and water. You can use undiluted vinegar for a really tough job. Use a stiff scrubbing brush to remove mildew in crevices. Dry the furniture well with rags, then set it in the sun to dry completely.

ON THE ROAD AGAIN

GLAD Zipper Bags have dozens of uses for travel. Here are just a few useful tips:

- Store liquid toiletries in sealed bags so they won't ruin clothes if they break or spill.
- Carry fresh diapers in a gallon-size GLAD Zipper bag, which doubles as an emergency changing mat and can also store the dirty diapers until you get to a trash receptacle.

If mud gunks up your golf cleats on rainy days, spray them with WD-40 before you hit the links.

A dab of Alberto VO5 Conditioning Hairdressing on a clean cloth will make the shafts of your golf clubs sparkle.

A spray of WD-40 in the sockets of your golf cleats will also keep them from rusting.

 Strengthen your grip for golf or tennis by keeping a Penn tennis ball handy and squeezing it every once in awhile.

Chapter 11

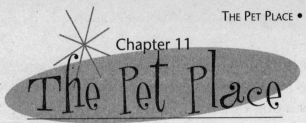

The Pet Place

These days it seems pets have as many supplies and accessories as children do. By the time you come back from the vet, you could be out a small fortune for ointments, treatments, and breath mints. You can save a bundle—and keep your pet healthier and happier—using ordinary products that are just as effective and often safer for pets and the environment. Here are the best tips we've found for keeping your furred, feathered, and floppy friends in tip-top shape.

GOOD GROOMING
All washed up

All out of pet shampoo? Just use your own Suave shampoo to wash the dog.

You can minimize the soap residue that remains after a dog's shampoo by adding some vinegar to the bath's rinse water. Then rinse the dog's coat again thoroughly with plain water.

A HEALTHY RINSE

After giving your pet a flea bath or a treatment for a skin infection, rinse its fur with a solution of vinegar and water (1 part vinegar to 3 parts water). Take care to keep the vinegar out of your pet's eyes.

To kill fleas found on your pet dog, use a little Dawn Dishwashing Detergent in the dog's bath. Make sure to rinse well with water afterward.

If your dog or cat doesn't like getting baths, try giving them dry baths instead. Just sprinkle baking soda over their fur, rub it in, and then brush out the baking soda.

You can also give your dog or cat a dry bath with cornstarch. Rub on the cornstarch, then brush it off. If you're careful, some pets will even let you vacuum the powder off!

 Give your kitty a special treatment with Johnson's Baby Powder. Rub it in, then brush it out for clean fur and a fresh smell.

Coat quality
Add 1 tablespoon vegetable oil to your dog's food every day to help eliminate dry, itchy skin.

Adding vegetable oil to pooch's dinner plate also helps slow down shedding.

BURRS BE GONE
Remove burrs from your dog's fur by crushing them with a pair of pliers and then pouring on a little Suave shampoo to loosen the pieces so you can remove them.

Another good burr-remover is vegetable oil, worked into the burrs. This also works for tar and other messes that Rover might have gotten into. Shampoo to remove the loosened gunk and oil.

 If your dog's fur gets tangled and matted, rub in some Alberto VO5 Conditioning Hairdressing, then brush with a stiff comb to remove the tangles.

What's in for pet's skin (and fur)

 If your dog's foot pads become dry and cracked, rub some Vaseline Petroleum Jelly into them. Remove excess with a soft cloth.

Alberto VO5 Conditioning Hairdressing also makes a good conditioner for a pet's pads.

If your dog has itchy skin, use vinegar as an after-shampoo treatment. Mix ½ cup vinegar into 1 gallon water and coat the dog's hair with the solution. Let it stay on the hair for 10 minutes, then rinse thoroughly. Protect the dog's eyes during this treatment.

PEST PREDICAMENTS

 When you have a flea infestation in your home, sprinkle your carpet or your rugs with salt to help kill any flea eggs. Let the salt sit for a few hours, then vacuum. Repeat every week for 6 weeks.

If your house or automobile gets "baptized" by a skunk, spray Febreze Fabric Spray around the smelly area to cover up the odor.

CURE THAT ODD HABIT

Dogs sometimes like to eat horse droppings in the barn. Some dog and horse owners claim that adding vinegar to the horse's feed, using ½ cup per feeding 2 times a day, will discourage dogs in this behavior.

Make your own flea repellent by slicing up a couple of lemons and boiling them in 1 quart water. Allow to cool, run through a strainer, and put in a spray bottle. Spray on pets as needed.

You can also kill fleas by adding 1 tablespoon Dawn Dish-  washing Detergent to a pan of water. Place the pan on the infested rug with a lamp shining down on the pan. Fleas will be drawn to the light, jump into the water, and drown.

 Put salt in your vacuum cleaner bag to help kill flea eggs that may be sucked up.

PET CARE 101
So long, stomach woes
To ease constipation in dogs, add 1 tablespoon vegetable oil to their dog food.

Add 1 tablespoon apple cider vinegar to your dog or cat's water bowl to improve overall health and digestion.

If your dog (not cat) seems to have an upset stomach, you can give it the same Pepto-Bismol you take. Give your pooch 1 tablespoon for every 20 pounds of weight, every 6 hours. This treatment can also be used to ease diarrhea in dogs.

Farewell, hairballs
To prevent hairballs, add 1 teaspoon vegetable oil to your cat's food every day.

 Another way to get a lubricant into your cat and prevent hairballs is to put a dab of Vaseline Petroleum Jelly on its nose. Cleanliness-conscious cats will lick their noses clean and get the lubricant into their systems that way.

These ideas are all ears
Floppy-eared dogs can be prone to yeast infections in their ears, especially after bathing or grooming. To avoid getting water in your dog's ears during a bath, plug its ears with cotton balls that have been moistened with apple cider vinegar.

Another ear-cleaning remedy is to mix
1 tablespoon vinegar, 1 tablespoon Rite
Aid hydrogen peroxide, 1 tablespoon
yucca root tea, 1 drop lavender oil, and
½ cup aloe vera gel. Apply to pet's ear
with Q-Tip Cotton Swabs, and clean out.

On the nose

If your dog comes home with a swollen
nose, most likely it's been stung by a
wasp. Bathe the sting area in vinegar to
ease the pain.

Keep an eye on it

For minor irritations in your pet's eyes, apply a
drop of vegetable oil in the corner of each eye.

If your cat or
dog has a dis-
charge from
their eyes, boil
a cup of dis-
tilled water with ¼ tea-
spoon salt. Allow this to
cool until just slightly
warm, then dab into the
corners of their eyes with
a cotton ball.

DOG-TIRED BONES

For an old dog's occa-
sional aches and pains,
mix some aspirin in
with its food, ¼ of a
tablet for every 15 to
20 pounds of weight,
once a day.

For minor skin irritations on pets, a tea bag, still warm from the cup (not hot) can be pressed against the area to provide relief.

Purrfect Cleaning Ideas
Oh no odors

If deodorizing kitty litter is too expensive for you, just buy a cheaper brand and mix in some baking soda to absorb odors.

When Rover romps with skunks and comes home fragrant, give him a tomato juice bath to kill the smell. Then top it off with a rinse of equal parts vinegar and water.

You can also remove skunk odors by rinsing your dog with undiluted vinegar. Keep the vinegar out of the dog's eyes for this process. The skunk smell will not totally dissipate but will be made bearable as it wears off.

Keep a Neater Litter Bin

Use vinegar to clean out a kitty litter pan. Remove the litter, pour in ½ inch of vinegar, and let it stand for 15 minutes. Pour out and dry the pan thoroughly, then sprinkle with baking soda and add fresh kitty litter.

If your pooch has been rolling in something that smells sweet to it but not to you, rub its coat with corn meal or baking soda, then brush it out.

Here's another odorific idea: Rub a smelly dog with a Downy Sheet to get rid of unpleasant aromas.

Eliminate odors in your pet's bedding by adding vinegar to the final rinse of your wash cycle. When the bedding is dry, sprinkle it with a little baking soda.

You can also use baking soda as a dry shampoo for bedding. Just sprinkle on, let it sit for awhile, and brush or vacuum up.

Urine trouble
Clean up urinary accidents from cats or dogs in your home by drying the area and then applying undiluted vinegar. The vinegar will help control the odor and keep the pet from visiting the area again.

Apply club soda to any carpeted area where a cat has urinated. Do not saturate. As the soda dries, it will neutralize the odor.

MAGIC HAIR REMOVER

Mix ¼ cup Final Touch fabric softener with water in a spray bottle, and spray it lightly on upholstered furniture where pet hair has accumulated. Do not saturate. When dry, vacuum off. You can also add fabric softener to your floor-cleaning water to help pick up stray pet hairs.

Another way to both absorb the wetness and neutralize the odor of pet urine is to generously sprinkle the spot with salt. Let dry overnight, then vacuum.

After cleaning up a pet accident on a rug or other area, spray it with a mixture of half water and half ammonia or lemon juice to hide the odor and discourage repeat visits.

Hair, there, and everywhere

To get rid of pet hair on fabric, rub the area with the very clean sole of a sneaker.

Pick up pet hair easily by wrapping your hand with any kind of adhesive tape, sticky side out. Run your hand along the upholstery and pick up the hair. A slightly dampened O-Cel-O sponge also works for picking up pet hair.

Rub a Downy Sheet across upholstered furniture and other places
where cat hair collects. The sheet
will attract the hair and make it easier to pick up.

Spray a coat or jacket with Static Guard, wait a
minute or two, then easily brush away any stuck-
on pet hairs.

PREVENTING PET PROBLEMS
Let's play keep-away
When training new puppies or cats, you might
be able to keep them off furniture by placing
pieces of Reynolds Wrap Aluminum Foil on the
 seat. The new pets won't like
the rustling sound and can be
broken of the habit.

If your cat likes nibbling on your houseplants,
keep it away from them by mixing 2 drops hot
sauce and 1 quart water. Let sit an hour, then
mist this onto plant leaves.

When you put out your trash in plastic bags, coat
the outside of the bags with a little ammonia.
The smell should keep strays away. Consider
spraying the outside of your trash cans with
ammonia, too.

Retrain a pet that likes to munch on electrical cords by wiping down the cords with Ivory liquid soap. One taste and your pet won't be back.

 You can keep cats away from no-cat zones in your home by sprinkling or spraying the areas lightly with vinegar.

Train a dog to stay away from your lidded garbage can by soaking an old sock in ammonia and tying it to the handle.

Stop barking!
Squirt full-strength lemon juice into your dog's mouth to discourage barking. Say, "Quiet!" as you do this so it gets the point.

Use the leg of a pair of No nonsense panty hose to muzzle your pet. Wrap it around the pet's jaw twice, then cross the ends below the chin. Bring the ends up behind the ears and tie it tightly. The fabric will stretch enough for comfort but not enough so the animal can bite.

IDEAS WITH HORSE SENSE
When your horse's mane becomes tangled and knotted, work some Alberto VO5 Conditioning Hairdressing into it to help with the detangling.

Use WD-40 to remove gum, tar, and other sticky substances from horse's hooves.

 You can shine your horses hooves by rubbing Alberto VO5 Conditioning Hairdressing on them.

Spruce up your horse's coat by adding ½ cup vinegar to 1 quart water. Use this in a spray bottle to spray the horse's coat before showing.

Pour ¼ cup apple cider vinegar onto a horse's regular grain feeding once a day to deter flies.

TOP TIPS FOR FISH

Clean aquarium accessories in a bowl with a Polident Denture Cleanser tablet added. Scrub and rinse well to remove anything harmful to the fish.

Brighten a fish tank by adding 1 or 2 drops food coloring to the water.

 Rub the inside glass of a fish tank with noniodized salt. Use a plastic pot scrubber to remove hard water deposits or other buildup. Rinse well before returning the fish to the tank.

Index

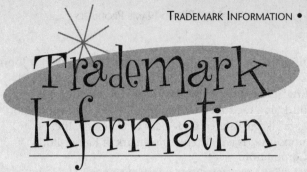

Trademark Information

"Alberto VO5" is a registered trademark of Alberto-Culver Company.

"Alka-Seltzer" is a registered trademark of Bayer Corporation.

"Blistex" is a registered trademark of Blistex Bracken Limited Partnership.

"Borax" is a registered trademark of U.S. Borax, Inc.

"Clorox" is a registered trademark of The Clorox Company.

"Crayola" is a registered trademark of Binney & Smith Properties, Inc.

"Cutex" is a registered trademark of The Cutex Company.

"Dawn" is a registered trademark of The Procter & Gamble Company.

"Diamond Matches" is a registered trademark of The Diamond Match Company.

"Dixie" is a registered trademark of Fort James Operating Company.

"Downy" is a registered trademark of The Procter & Gamble Company.

"Electrasol" is a registered trademark of Reckitt Benckiser, Inc.

"Elmer's" is a registered trademark of The Borden Company.

"Febreze" is a registered trademark of The Procter & Gamble Company.

"Final Touch" is a registered trademark of Lever Brothers Company.

"Finesse" is a registered trademark of Helene Curtis Industries, Inc.

"Fresh Step" is a registered trademark of The Clorox Company.

"Gillette" is a registered trademark of The Gillette Company.

"GLAD" is a registered trademark of Union Carbide Corporation.

"Griffin" is a registered trademark of Hickory Brands, Inc.

"Ivory" is a registered trademark of The Procter & Gamble Company.

"Johnson's Baby" is a registered trademark of Johnson & Johnson.

"Krazy Glue" is a registered trademark of Toagosei Co., Ltd.

"Melitta" is a registered trademark of Horst Wolfgang Bentz.

"Mobil 1" is a registered trademark of Mobil Oil Corporation.

"Niagara" is a registered trademark of Conopco, Inc.

"No nonsense" is a registered trademark of Kayser-Roth Corporation.

"O-Cel-O" is a registered trademark of General Mills, Inc.

"Pam" is a registered trademark of Gibraltar Industries, Inc.

"Pampers" is a registered trademark of The Procter & Gamble Company.

"Pepto-Bismol" is a registered trademark of The Norwich Pharmacal Company.

"Penn" is a registered trademark of Penn Racquet Sports, Inc.

"Pepsodent" is a registered trademark of The Pepsodent Co.

"Phillips' Milk of Magnesia" is a registered trademark of Chas. H. Phillips Chemical Co.

"Pledge" is a registered trademark of S. C. Johnson & Son, Inc.

"Polident" is a registered trademark of Wernet Dental Mfg. Co., Inc.

"Post-it" is a registered trademark of 3M Company.

"Q-Tips" is a registered trademark of Q-Tips, Inc.

"Reach" is a registered trademark of Johnson & Johnson.

"Revlon" is a registered trademark of Revlon, Inc.

"Reynolds," "Reynolds Wrap," and "Cut-Rite" are registered trademarks of Reynolds Metals Company.

"Rite Aid" is a registered trademark of Rite Aid Corporation.

"Scope" is a registered trademark of The Procter & Gamble Company.

"Scott" is a registered trademark of Scott Paper Company.

"Simoniz" is a registered trademark of Simoniz Company.

"Static Guard" is a registered trademark of Alberto-Culver Company.

"Suave" is a registered trademark of Helene Curtis, Inc.

"Tide" is a registered trademark of The Procter & Gamble Company.

"Vaseline" is a registered trademark of Chesebrough-Pond's Inc.

"WD-40" is a registered trademark of WD-40 Company, Inc.